A Simple Introduction to Capital Expenditure Decisions

IRFAN

A Simple Introduction to Capital Expenditure Decisions

Douglas Garbutt, A.C.I.S. A.C.W.A. Dip.Ed.(Lond.)

Department of Production and Industrial Administration
College of Aeronautics, Cranfield, Bedfordshire

London Sir Isaac Pitman and Sons Ltd

First published 1967

SIR ISAAC PITMAN AND SONS LTD.
PITMAN HOUSE, PARKER STREET, KINGSWAY, LONDON, W.C.2
THE PITMAN PRESS, BATH
PITMAN HOUSE, BOUVERIE STREET, CARLTON, MELBOURNE
P.O. BOX 7721, JOHANNESBURG, TRANSVAAL
P.O. BOX 6038, PORTAL STREET, NAIROBI, KENYA

ASSOCIATED COMPANIES
PITMAN MEDICAL PUBLISHING COMPANY LTD.
46 CHARLOTTE STREET, LONDON, W.1
PITMAN PUBLISHING CORPORATION
20 EAST 46TH STREET, NEW YORK, N.Y. 10017
SIR ISAAC PITMAN (CANADA) LTD.
(INCORPORATING THE COMMERCIAL TEXT BOOK COMPANY)
PITMAN HOUSE, 381–383 CHURCH STREET, TORONTO

SBN: 273 41173 x

Made in Great Britain at the Pitman Press, Bath
F7

To Betty

Preface

THIS book arose from my teaching at Cranfield and previously at the Polytechnic, Regent Street, when I became aware of the need for a simple introduction to "discounted cash flow."

The book explores, also, the accounting and other measures of profitability, such as the pay-out plot, since many students and managers come to D.C.F. with set ideas about profitability and they need to be shown how and why these other measures are inadequate if, indeed, they are. Each measure is considered on its merits and, hopefully, the superiority of the discounting approach is demonstrated. In general, practical and simple examples are used and, at the end of the book, there are forty-three self-examination questions.

I would like to express my appreciation and gratitude to Professor Pearson Hunt of Harvard University and Leonard Kingshott of the Ford Motor Company who first stimulated my interest in this topic and to Ray Reul of F.M.C. who taught me a great deal. My indebtedness to them is evident in the book but they bear no responsibility for its failings.

D.G.

Contents

1 *The Need for Evaluation of Costs, Profits and Capital Expenditure*

MODERN industry, both in Britain and overseas, is subject to certain tendencies which make the sound evaluation of costs, profits and capital investments much more urgent than has been the case in the past.

SCALE OF BUSINESS

First of all the scale of enterprises in business is increasing and so the capital commitments on individual projects are tending to rise.

TAXATION

The high rates of taxation which apply in most countries and the difficulties of computing many tax allowances, which may vary widely according to circumstances, means that taxation has become an important factor in business decisions. After all, the business man must be interested primarily in the cash which remains in hand after a project has come to a successful conclusion and after the tax man has had his share. The timing of tax-collection is also important because there may be considerable delays between incurring liability to tax and the actual payment of the tax. This means that many businesses have, in effect, funds which are still "on loan" to them from the Inland Revenue.

COMPETITIVE PRESSURES

The growing scale of industrial enterprise has also had the effect of increasing the competitive pressure on margins of profit. This may be coupled with the fact that capital is fairly readily available at a reasonable cost so that businesses with reasonable prospects of future profit have little difficulty in raising funds. In fact, in some ways, the availability of funds may be a snare and a delusion if it leads a business into recruiting funds at the least advantageous cost, or undertaking unprofitable ventures.

EVALUATION TECHNIQUES

For these reasons academics and business consultants have been looking more closely at the techniques which are available for evaluating expenditures and profits. Current thinking is that many of the techniques used in the past are not effective and can be misleading in many circumstances.

Basically, this book advocates the use of the discounted-cash-flow method, although it looks closely at other methods and attempts to indicate the limits of their usefulness.

THE GENERAL BACKGROUND TO CAPITAL EXPENDITURE DECISIONS

PLANS AND POLICIES

When a company is considering capital expenditure decisions it must attempt, first of all, to fit a new decision into its long-term plans and development policy. It is no use an oil company going for expenditure in, for instance, ice-cream manufacture unless it has seriously considered the implications of entering a new kind of market. It may be that a policy which appears not so profitable in the short term may be the one which will best serve the long-term policies of the company.

ALTERNATIVES

A company must also consider all the available alternatives which are open to it. A decision which is based on too few alternatives may be highly misleading. These alternatives may be technological, that is, there may be new ways of doing the same thing, or new technologies coming along which offer new opportunities for a company which is in a declining market. There are always opportunities, too, for new markets and new products. The firm must closely investigate which, if any, of these may be available to it. Finally, a firm has various economic alternatives: perhaps different ways of financing the same project. These, as far as possible, must be considered in quantitative terms. This book indicates the methods which may be used for evaluating alternatives of an economic nature.

RISKS, UNCERTAINTIES AND INTANGIBLES

The most difficult part of making capital expenditure decisions may be evaluating the risks, uncertainties and intangibles in a decision. Long business experience may give certain executives a "hunch" insight into the risks, uncertainties and intangibles which any particular project faces. This does not mean, however, that the effort of trying to identify these factors or to express them in terms of numbers is a waste of time. First it is necessary to distinguish, sharply, between the three factors.

RISK

Risk will exist when each alternative facing the business man will give a set of possible outcomes and it is possible to put a probability on each of the results.

UNCERTAINTY

We may talk about uncertainty when we cannot assess the probability of the different alternatives or when we are rather uncertain as to the probabilities. For instance, if we know that in drilling for gas in the North Sea there is a one in forty chance of hitting gas, then we know the conditions of risk. If, however, we have no experience of what the probabilities are, then the conditions are uncertain.

All business economic problems are subject to risk and uncertainty. Whilst no technique of evaluation can eliminate risk, it is possible to use techniques which incorporate it into an evaluation.

INTANGIBLES

No business decisions will be made in terms of cost alone. Having analysed the cost and profit to be made from capital expenditure, a business man will always take into account other factors such as political and social conditions. These may be powerful but they are intangible. Consideration of intangibles may mean that the business man sometimes takes a decision which appears disadvantageous in cost terms. This may be perfectly justified if he is right in his evaluation of the intangibles.

The accountant and economist need to avoid the error of believing that the figures of cost and capital expenditure give the decision to be made in all circumstances. The figures, in fact, indicate the economic evaluation. The final decision must be based on a business evaluation.

COMPANY PROFITABILITY

First let us state the obvious: a company has made a profit only if and when it has first recovered the capital and costs which it incurred in making and selling its products. The first requirement of company activity must therefore be to cover its costs and to achieve capital recovery. Beyond this it needs to show profitability.

This profitability can be looked at in two ways: firstly, in terms of the *profit earnings*. These earnings are calculated by taking the sales revenue of the firm and deducting from the sales revenue, in a particular period, the costs of the goods sold plus a proportion of the expenses of the period over which the revenues were earned. The operating profit which remains may be regarded as the basic earnings from which a reward will be paid to the various kinds of capital which have contributed funds to the business.

The alternative way of looking at company profitability is to look at the *cash generated* by the company. The cash generation will be calculated by taking the reported profit and adding back any items which do not represent a flow of cash in the current year. For example, depreciation is not a cash flow but is simply a charge of a proportion of the costs of fixed assets which were paid for in cash in earlier years. Items such as interest and dividend payments to the different categories of capital and taxation which *do* represent cash payments are deducted and the resultant figure shows the cash generated by a company and available for capital expenditure in the current period of account.

These definitions can be best illustrated by an example.

EARNINGS

British companies are not obliged to report their sales figures in their annual accounts, but some companies do so.

The Steel Company of Wales is one which does, and the

following statement has been prepared from information in their annual report on 30th September, 1961—

		£(000s)
Turnover (sales revenue)		133,040
Operating costs (cost of goods sold and expenses of period)	£109,788	
Depreciation	8,333	
		118,121
Operating profit		14,919
Fixed asset replacement reserve		2,000
EARNINGS BEFORE INTEREST AND TAX		12,919
Interest	4,890	
Tax provision	3,100	
		7,990
Balance of profit		4,929
Dividends		2,450
RETAINED EARNINGS		£2,479

In this presentation, operating costs and depreciation are deducted from sales turnover to show the operating profit of £14,919,000.

From this a reserve of £2 million has been put aside for replacement of assets, leaving earnings after payment of interest and tax of £7,990,000. The balance of profit is available to shareholders: £2,450,000 has been paid out in dividends and £2,479,000, the balance of retained earnings, has been "ploughed back" and represents investment in the company by the shareholders.

CASH GENERATION

It is possible to calculate the generation of cash from a number of starting points, but perhaps the simplest is to start with the final figure of retained earnings of £2,479,000.

Each successive item can then be considered: does it or does it not represent a payment of cash? If it does *not* represent a cash payment, then it will be added back.

The items which represent cash payments are—

	£(000s)
Dividends	2,450
Tax	3,100
Interest	4,890
Operating costs	109,788
These total	£120,228

The calculation of cash generation is therefore—

	£(000s)
Turnover	133,040
less cash items	120,228
Cash generation	£12,812

This could also be calculated by adding back the non-cash items to the retained earnings—

		£(000s)
Retained earnings		2,479
Add back		
Fixed asset replacement reserve .	2,000	
Depreciation	8,333	
		10,333
Cash generation		£12,812

From a technical point of view, these calculations can be criticized. For instance, the tax provided for in the current year is rarely actually paid in that year. Managers with access to full internal information within their companies would obtain more accurate data on cash generation. Outsiders relying on the published information can only obtain an approximate figure from the above calculations.

No company can afford to base its financial management entirely on earnings or cash generation. It must set its financial policy so as to take account of both of these approaches to evaluation of its results.

THE REQUIREMENTS FOR EARNINGS

What then are the requirements for earnings? How much should a company earn?

1. *Growth*

The first requirement of company profitability is that capital must be provided for the growth of the company over time. This capital may be obtained by reinvestment of earnings made by the firm or it may be obtained in various ways from the capital market and other sources.

2. *Maintenance of Dividends*

The availability of capital from the capital market and other sources will depend, to some extent, on the way in which the company has rewarded its existing shareholders. A fair return to existing shareholders in the light of current market conditions will mean that investors will be prepared to invest fresh capital in the company should it come to the market for these funds. Unless a company pays sufficient dividends to maintain the value of its shares in the Stock Market it may prove very difficult to attract new capital on the free market when it is required.

3. *Payment of Debt*

In a similar way the earnings of a company must enable the interest charges on debts, as they occur over the year, to be paid. Interest charges are payable whether the company is profitable or not. Failure to earn sufficient to meet the interest charges will mean that a company reports a loss for the period.

4. *Provision for Cover*

The Stock Market also looks to earnings which provide a "cover," that is, an element of profit which is retained in the business and which implies that the capital of the business is growing over the years. Not all industries retain the same amount of earnings for growth.

THE REQUIREMENTS FOR CASH GENERATION

Since earnings and cash generation are related (although rarely identical) figures, it follows that the requirements for cash generation will be similar.

Debt Service and Dividends

The cash generated by a company must be sufficient to ensure payment of all interest charges due to debenture holders and also to provide sufficient cash for dividends to preference and ordinary shareholders.

Redemption of Debt

The cash must also be generated which will eventually ensure the redemption of debts. A company may have a twenty-year debenture falling due in five years' time. Stock-market analysts will study its cash generation closely in an attempt to gauge whether a company will in fact be able to meet its obligations. It may be argued that a company which is obliged to "fund" may find itself in a difficult position and have to pay more for its funds than a company which has the alternative left to it of redeeming the debt out of its own funds.

Capital Expenditure

Obviously it is from cash generation that the company provides, to a large extent, for investment in and replacement of fixed assets. It must also find working capital to finance the acquisition of working stocks or to enable credit to be given to customers. Top management always has fresh funds coming to hand: it always has, therefore, the problem of capital expenditure before it.

THE CAPITAL INVESTMENT SITUATION

Figure 1/1 shows, in diagrammatic form, the situation which faces top management on capital investment in practice.

In the centre, top management is the key group of people in the capital investment situation. It has an access to a supply of

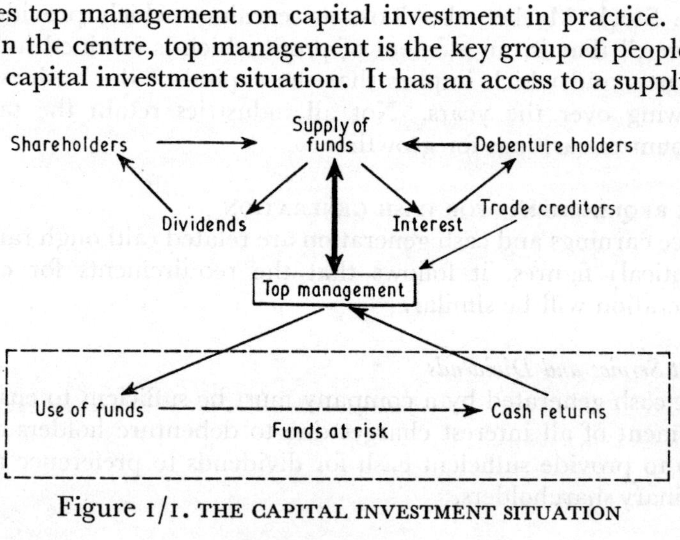

Figure 1/1. THE CAPITAL INVESTMENT SITUATION

funds which may come from shareholders on the one hand, or from debenture holders on the other.

USE OF FUNDS

Receiving the supply of funds, top management puts these

to use. It decides to build new plant or to invest in research and development or to provide funds for establishing welfare or other facilities. Whatever the actual decision may be in physical terms it will always, in management terms, involve the use of funds. This means that hard cash is paid out for facilities and other services, such as the use of labour and rent and rates.

FUNDS AT RISK

The funds are at risk and it is hoped that they will eventually result in cash returns, but the line between use of funds and cash returns is dotted because it is not certain, by any means, that there will be any returns for the company.

CASH RETURNS

If the cash does return, however, it returns into the hands of top management, who may, as stated above, put the returns to fresh use in which case a capital expenditure decision must be made. A proportion of the returns, however, must go back to the suppliers: that is, in payment of dividends to shareholders and interest to debenture holders and in repayment of borrowing.

TRADE CREDIT

Management can obtain trade credit on a short-term basis. This may be an important source of funds in certain trades but it is always a dangerous source since it results in short-term demands for cash. Prudent management will always restrict the use of trade credit within limits which allow the discharge of the trade credit within the terms given, usually one month or two at the most.

Figure 1/1 summarizes the situation in which the top management of every firm finds itself: financially, it is responsible for controlling and maintaining the supply of funds. This supply must be put to use, and management must consider alternative uses and decide which, if any, of these uses offers most potential advantage to the firm.

Some business men argue that they do not have capital expenditure problems. They say that whenever they have to spend money on fixed investments they have no alternative but to do so. This attitude of mind is mistaken. Whilst it is true that management may sometimes find itself with no alternative, this is the exceptional case. Even when there is only one available use for funds, management must consider what earnings that use will provide. If a business cannot earn more for the investor than he can obtain from fixed interest securities, then it should liquidate and return the funds to the investor.

Every business must be concerned with evaluating its financial results. It must know what its existing profitability is and it must know what the results of its future actions will be on that profitability.

EVALUATING CAPITAL EXPENDITURE

Every business, therefore, needs methods of evaluating capital expenditures which enable it to discriminate clearly between alternative proposals for the use of funds. Is it better to spend £10,000 on a new milling machine or on a new filing system? Should the company be spending all the cash which comes into its coffers or should it be investing funds outside the business for "a rainy day"? Is it better to install a new filing system or is it better to spend the £10,000 on using a consultant? Top management requires a yardstick which will discriminate between alternative proposals and the different ways that there may be of implementing them.

PROFITABILITY AND EVALUATION

Top management must also be concerned with the question, what will be the effect of a new project on the overall rate of return of the business? If a company has shown over the years a 10 per cent profitability after tax, and this has proved to be a rate of return that gives a satisfactory rate of dividend to shareholders, will a new project be sufficient to keep that profitability up?

ACCOUNTS AND EVALUATION

The big problem which worries many business men is the reconciling of the measures which they use for evaluating investment with the statements and returns which are provided by the accountant. Because these returns and statements are incorporated in company legislation, they are naturally an important component in thinking about profitability. If a theory is advanced that a particular way of evaluation will result in higher profits, then management wants to know that this will in fact eventually result in a profit for the shareholders as shown in the company's annual accounts. Unfortunately many of the yardsticks for company investment which are suggested do not tie up very immediately with the accountancy statement and some caution is needed before applying these methods.

No single yardstick of investment is available which will give an easy reconciliation between the method and the accounting measures or indicate the effect on the overall rate of return on the business whilst at the same time discriminating between alternatives and the different ways of implementing them.

TWO APPROACHES

In this book a distinction is drawn between two kinds of evaluation—

1. *The going-concern evaluation.* This is the accounting method and is based on the past records of performance of a company.
2. *New project evaluation.* This involves using various discounted cash flow methods and is based on the future possibilities of the company.

Are these two not eventually reconcilable? Only in very broad terms, and, generally, estimates of profitability using accountancy methods will differ from estimates using the other methods. We will attempt to show that the application of the accountancy methods to the future possibilities may be highly deceptive and can lead to incorrect evaluations. This does not mean, however, that the accountancy methods are incorrect. They report the profitability of a firm over a previous period. Where contracts extend over a long period the accounts are concerned with reporting a fair amount of profit in interim periods.

The reported results of a company are deservedly considered important for they are the net outcome of many projects which the company has undertaken, some of which have been successful, some of which have been unsuccessful. The accounting returns show clearly the net result which has been achieved over a period. They are, however, one component only in the process of assessing future possibilities.

The assessment of new projects is, in some ways, simpler in that one particular project can be isolated for consideration. In other ways it is more difficult since we are looking into the future and trying to guess the outcome of actions taken at the present.

In the next chapter we look at the way in which the accountant assesses the return on investment. This is the going-concern method of assessment and it has very many practical values in day-to-day business. In succeeding chapters we look at new project evaluation and the way in which return on investment can be assessed in relation to specific projects. A great deal of confusion is created by criticisms of these two methods of evaluation, e.g. the accountants criticizing economists who propose the use of more satisfactory methods and economists criticizing accountants for "out of date thinking." In fact these two methods are answering different questions. Unsatisfactory as the accounting measures are in many ways, there is at present no viable substitute for them.

2 *Return on Investment—the Going-concern Evaluation*

ASSESSMENT of the profitability of a company on the going-concern basis is made by relating the profit for a period to the capital employed—

$$\frac{\text{Net profit}}{\text{Capital employed}} \times 100 = \text{Profitability per cent}$$

To illustrate the various computations of profitability, we have taken the published accounts of Selincourt and Sons Ltd. for the period ended 31st January, 1964, and the Balance Sheet at that date. The figures have been slightly simplified. The Balance Sheet is shown below.

CONSOLIDATED BALANCE SHEET OF SELINCOURT AND SONS LTD.
AS AT 31ST JANUARY, 1964 (simplified)

		£(000s)
EMPLOYMENT OF CAPITAL		
Fixed assets (at cost or valuation less depreciation and mortgages)		6,417
Investments		68
Current assets	5,269	
less Current liabilities and provisions	2,779	
Excess of current assets over current liabilities		2,490
NET ASSETS		8,975
Deduct 1964–5 income tax		513
TOTAL CAPITAL EMPLOYED		£8,462
DETAILS OF CAPITAL EMPLOYED		
Subscribed by members		
7% preference stock		125
1s. ordinary shares		1,726
Share premium		2,435
		4,286
Undistributed profits		
Capital reserves	261	
Revenue reserves	336	
		597
Capital and reserves applicable to members		4,883
Minority shareholders		389
6½% Convertible Loan Stock		3,190
TOTAL CAPITAL EMPLOYED		£8,462

The first point to notice is that the Balance Sheet has been arranged to show a figure "Total capital employed." This is the amount of assets provided by long-term funds and corresponds to the I.C.W.A. definition of total employment of capital.

Since there are no generally accepted definitions of these terms, the reader is warned to check all the data to satisfy himself which capital basis is, in fact, being used.

Making the calculations of the capital on various bases suggested, we get the following results—

1. *Total assets.* (This figure is the total of all the assets shown in the Balance Sheet.)

	£(000s)
Fixed assets	6,417
Investments	68
Current assets	5,269
Total assets	11,754

The total assets are, therefore, a little under £12 million.

2. *Total assets employed.* Here, those assets which are idle or excess to requirements in the period are eliminated. Let us assume in this case that the investment should be eliminated since these are assets employed outside the group. In an expanding group, it could very well be that some of the fixed assets would also be excess to requirements. A holding company often acquires subsidiaries, part of which it is intended to integrate into the group, part of which it is intended to dispose of. Such assets, held pending disposal, would be eliminated from the capital base.

However, the calculation shows—

	£(000s)
Fixed assets	6,417
Current assets	5,269
Total assets employed . .	11,686

3. *Assets provided by long-term funds.* This is the figure which the original presentation was intended to bring out—it is £8,462,000.

The two methods of calculation can be seen in each half of the Balance Sheet.

Part I shows the use of funds.

		£(000s)
Fixed assets		6,417
Investment		68
Current assets		5,269
		11,754
less Current liabilities and provisions	2,779	
Income tax	513	
		3,292
ASSETS PROVIDED BY LONG-TERM FUNDS		£8,462

Part II shows the sources of funds.

Preference stock	125
Ordinary shares	1,726
Reserves	2,435
Share premium	261
Other capital reserves	336
Revenue reserves	
Minority shareholders	389
Convertible loan stock	3,190
ASSETS PROVIDED BY LONG-TERM FUNDS .	£8,462

Part I corresponds to the "assets side" of the Balance Sheet and Part II to the "liabilities side."

4. *Assets provided by ordinary shareholders (stockholders' equity).* Since Selincourt is a holding company which controls a large number of smaller companies, there are some shareholders remaining with a direct share in subsidiaries. These are shown in the Balance Sheet as Minority shareholders. From the point of view of the holding company they are outsiders, providing long-term funds but not sharing in the equity of the holding company itself.

The preference stock carries a right to 7 per cent dividend each year from profits before any dividends can be paid to ordinary shares. Preference shares are usually entitled to preference on dissolution of the company, also. If this be the case such shares or stock carry no rights to participate in the distribution of any surpluses apart from what may be due to them by way of accumulated dividends.

It is on this basis that we calculate the ordinary shareholders' interest—

	£(000s)
1s. Ordinary shares	1,726
Reserves	
Share premium	2,435
Other capital reserves	261
Revenue reserves	336
	£4,758

This interest can also be calculated by taking total assets less all liabilities and preference capital—

		£(000s)
Total assets		11,754
less Current liabilities	2,779	
Taxation	513	
Preference shares	125	
Minority interest	389	
Loan stock	3,190	
		6,996
		£4,758

Notice that in confining this definition of shareholders interest to ordinary shareholders, we have implicitly treated preference shareholders in much the same way as the debenture or loan stock holders, i.e. as lenders to the company, rather than as ownership interest.

This is at variance, again, with the approach of the Selincourt Company which has grouped preference and ordinary shareholders together.

Legally, the latter approach is more correct, since the owners of preference shares as shareholders are not entitled to their dividend unless profits are available. Debenture holders as lenders are entitled to their interest whether a profit is made or not! Failure to pay debenture interest can lead directly to the winding up of the company by the debenture holders.

Nevertheless, financially, the residual risks of the company lie with the ordinary shareholders, and it is more common to calculate this profitability in relation to ordinary shares than in relation to all shares.

Later, in the treatment of gearing, the same reasoning is followed: preference shares and debentures are grouped together as fixed reward capital.

THE DEFINITION OF PROFITS

In general, the definition of profit must be related to the capital base to which that profit will be related in calculating profitability.

"Profit" is a word having a wide variety of meanings. In accountancy, the profits for a year will be the total income from sales, less the costs charged against those profits in the period. These costs normally include such items as depreciation which represent costs held in suspense and charged to production on an equitable basis such as calculations of anticipated wear and tear and future life.

THE EFFECT OF DEPRECIATION

In cases where depreciation charges have been insufficient to recover the cost of an asset over its life, there will be a loss on the eventual disposal of the plant which ought logically to be charged against the profits of previous years but which, in practice, is usually charged against the profits of the current year. Less logically, such losses, if exceptionally large, may be put in suspense and charged against the profits of future years.

There is no legal obligation for companies to charge depreciation on their assets against their profits but, of course, if they do not do so, there will be no preservation of the capital in the business. A depreciation charge represents a recovery of part of the capital and any surplus remaining is true profit in the sense of a surplus return over and above the original investment (always assuming that the life of the investment covers the full term anticipated).

Depreciation is calculated by taking the original cost of a machine, say £10,000 and estimating how long it will be in use and what value it will have on disposal at the end of its life. If at the end of ten years we can sell the asset for £1,000 then we can say that depreciation has been £9,000, that is £900 per year over ten years.

If the machine were the only asset held, and it earned revenues of £3,000 per annum, then the accounting profits would be reported each year as shown in the table on page 18.

			Annual Earnings	Depreciation	Accounting Profit
		£	£	£	£
Time 0	Investment	10,000	—	—	—
Year 1			3,000	900	2,100
Year 2			3,000	900	2,100
Year 3			3,000	900	2,100
Year 4			3,000	900	2,100
Year 5			3,000	900	2,100
Year 6			3,000	900	2,100
Year 7			3,000	900	2,100
Year 8			3,000	900	2,100
Year 9			3,000	900	2,100
Year 10			3,000	900	2,100

If the estimates of life or disposal value of the asset are incorrect, then the profits reported in the early years will prove to have been incorrect. Suppose, in the example, the asset is disposed of at the end of three years for £1,000.

The table below shows the results—

			Annual Earnings	Depreciation or Loss	Accounting Profit or Loss
		£	£	£	£
Time 0	Investment	10,000			
Year 1			3,000	900	2,100
Year 2			3,000	900	2,100
Year 3			3,000	900	2,100
					Profits 6,300
Equipment sold for		1,000		Loss 6,300	Loss 6,300
Total cost of asset		9,000		9,000	Nil

The position, looking back, may be summarized by saying that using the asset cost £9,000 (original cost less disposal value). The earnings it brought in were £3,000 per annum for three years: £9,000. The project, therefore, showed neither a loss nor a profit.

However, because of our expectations, this was reported to shareholders for three years as a profit of £2,100 (total £6,300), followed by a loss in the final year of £6,300.

Directors are obliged to disclose in their annual report and accounts the amounts, if any, set aside in any year in respect of depreciation.

NON-TRADING PROFITS

They must also disclose income received from dividends, interest and other non-trading activities. Where unusual profits have been made in one year, these will be excluded from all the calculations of profitability. It would be unsound to include in current income the profit from sale of land and buildings where this is not the normal business of the firm. If this were done, any comparisons of profitability would be highly misleading.

Similarly, where investments are eliminated from the gross assets to give the gross assets employed, then the corresponding dividends and interest received will be deducted from the profits for the year.

On the other hand, the interest paid to debentures will only be deducted from income when the return to shareholders' equity is being calculated. In all other cases the funds provided by debenture holders are included in the capital base and the return must include any payments to debenture holders. A similar logic applies to the inclusion or exclusion of preference shares and their dividends.

TREATMENT OF TAXATION

The most difficult problem is the treatment of taxation. Some taxes such as rates (which are local taxes related to occupancy of land and buildings) are treated as costs. Income-tax and profits tax in the past and corporation and income-tax at the moment represent taxes which are calculated, in some measure, to the profits currently earned by the company.

It would appear most logical to take profits after deduction of tax because the residue would represent the net amount left in the hands of the company or the shareholder. Unfortunately, however, the timing of tax payments has been such that, depending on the accounting year adopted, companies of similar status and profit-earning capacity might be paying taxes for the same period at vastly differing times. Such allowances as the capital allowance on plant and equipment may also differ according to the location of the companies and the dates on which they acquired the assets. Finally, whilst most companies follow the practice of providing for the future taxes which will arise on their current profits, some companies still provide only for those taxes which are currently payable.

The result of all these factors, which are by no means a comprehensive account of the problems, is that the after-tax profits are generally considered a less reliable guide than the profits gross of tax. Whether the advent of Corporation tax will simplify the position remains to be seen.

DEFINING PROFITS

To illustrate the calculation of related profits, the Consolidated Profit and Loss Account of Selincourt and Sons Ltd. for the thirteen months ended 31st January, 1964, is shown below.

RETURN ON INVESTMENT—GOING-CONCERN BASIS

DEFINING INCOME

CONSOLIDATED PROFIT AND LOSS ACCOUNTS OF SELINCOURT AND SONS LTD.

for 13 months ended 31st January, 1964

		£(000s)
Group trading profit		1,409
add investment income . . .		8
		1,417
less depreciation		170
		1,247
less interest on 6½% Loan Stock .	111	
less taxation	566	
		677
		570
add balances brought forward . .	93	
deduct minority interests . . .	110	
		17
AVAILABLE FOR APPROPRIATION . .		553

The statement has been drawn up so as to show the amount of profits (£553,000) which is available for appropriation to the shareholders of the holding company. In fact, the taxation arising on the profits would also be regarded as an appropriation although in this case it has already been deducted.

Payment of the debenture interest is not an appropriation of profit, since it is chargeable whether profits are made or not.

The balance brought forward would be any amount remaining in the profit and loss account from previous years.

Since the profit and loss account is consolidated, it includes the profits of the holding company and of the subsidiaries and, therefore, the entitlement of the minority shareholders to profits has been deducted before showing the final figure of profits for appropriation to the shareholders of the holding company.

In appropriating these profits, the directors may decide upon the dividends which can be paid, but will also set aside amounts to be retained in the form of reserves.

A final point to be noted is that the accounts cover a thirteen month period. Normally accounts cover a twelve month period but it is not unusual for a slightly longer period to be taken if, for instance a group is establishing a common accounting date for all its subsidiaries. A group cannot, of course, do this too often: it is in the nature of an adjustment period.

For comparison purposes, therefore, it seems best to reduce the figures by one-thirteenth so as to calculate profitability on a twelve-month basis. Comparisons with previous years can thus be made with a greater degree of accuracy.

The table below shows the calculation of profitability on each capital base—

1. *Total Assets.* The capital base is £11,754,000. The related income, before tax but after depreciation, is £1,247,000 less one-thirteenth, or £96,000, that is £1,151,000.

2. *Total Assets Employed.* The capital base is £11,686. The related income is £1,247,000 less £8,000 investment income, leaving £1,239,000. This is reduced by one-thirteenth, £95,000 to leave £1,144,000.

3. *Assets Provided by Long-term Funds.* The capital base is £8,462,000 and the related income is the same as is taken for the total assets, £1,151,000.

4. *Assets Provided by Ordinary Shareholders.* The capital base is £4,758. The related income is more tricky to calculate, but, briefly, the procedure is to eliminate any income attributable to other interests providing long-term funds.

These are interest on loan stock £111 and minority interests, £110. Interest on loan stock is shown in the accounts gross and needs no adjustment. The minority interest, however, represents a portion of the profits after the tax of £566 has been deducted. Part of that tax relates to the minority interest.

Also, the profits brought forward from previous years must, as in the previous calculations, be ignored.

We are left with the following calculation—

	£
Profits for the thirteen months	1,247,000
less interest on loan stock	111,000
Profits attributable to minority and holding company	1,136,000
Deduct minority interest $\left(\frac{110}{570} \times 1{,}136\right)$	219,000
Before tax profits attributable to holding company	£917,000

This must be reduced by one-thirteenth, £70,000, to give the profit figure of £847,000.

The rates of return shown by each method can be summarized as follows—

Capital Base	Capital £(000s)	Profits £(000s)	% Return on Investment
1. Total assets	11,754	1,151	9·8
2. Total assets employed . .	11,686	1,144	9·8
3. Assets provided by long-term funds	8,462	1,151	13·6
4. Assets provided by ordinary shareholders	4,758	847	17·8

All figures have been approximated and dealt with in £000s.

What interpretation can be placed on these rates of return? Obviously, if we adopt the same definitions of capital and income for past or in future years, then we will have a yardstick of the success of our investment, whichever capital base is used.

In the example taken, there is no significant difference between the first and second bases. The investments and their related income made little difference to the rate of return.

There is a big difference, however, between these first two ratios and the second two.

The first reason for this is that the return to long-term funds has eliminated short-term borrowing from trade creditors from the capital base. The result is striking and shows the importance of the capital obtained without interest charges or dividend payments.

The further increase in profitability to ordinary shareholders which is 17·8 per cent is due to the use of gearing. Since the use of gearing is an important aspect of financial management, it warrants further attention.

GEARING

Gearing, or in American terms, leverage, means the financing of a company in part by the issue of fixed interest capital. For this purpose, debentures which carry fixed interest may be grouped with preference shares which claim a fixed percentage dividend which has priority over dividends to ordinary shares.

The tax disadvantage imposed on preference shares by Corporation tax makes it highly unlikely that many preference shares will be issued in the future.

The effect of gearing can be illustrated by the following data concerning two companies, A and B. They have identical earnings records but they have different proportions of gearing.

		LONG-TERM CAPITALIZATION	
		5% Debentures	Ordinary Shares (plus retained earnings)
		£(000s)	£(000s)
Company A	High gearing	100	100
Company B	Low gearing	40	160

Earnings Record		Total Profits	Debenture Interest	Ordinary Share Earnings	
		£(000s)	£(000s)	£(000s)	%
19–1	(A)	10	5	5	5
	(B)	10	2	8	5
19–2	(A)	5	5	0	0
	(B)	5	2	3	1·875
19–3	(A)	20	5	15	15
	(B)	20	2	18	11·25
19–4	(A)	40	5	35	35
	(B)	40	2	38	23·7

It can be seen that each company has a capital of £200. Company A gears high by taking 50 per cent of its long-term funds from a 5 per cent debenture. Company B gears low by taking only 20 per cent of its long-term funds from a debenture.

The first year, 19–1 is a fair year in which each company earns £10,000. Company A must pay £5,000 debenture interest, being 5 per cent on £100,000. This leaves £5,000 to ordinary shares of £100,000, which is earnings of 5 per cent.

Company B only pays £2,000 debenture interest, being 5 per cent on £40,000, leaving £8,000 to ordinary shares of £160,000.

The second year 19–2 is a poor year, in which each company earns only £5,000. For Company A, this is sufficient only to meet the interest charges, leaving no profits at all for the ordinary shareholders. Company B, with its lower gearing is able to meet its interest charges of £2,000 and is left with £3,000 earnings for equity, which is a return of 1·875 per cent.

In a bad year, then, the ordinary shareholders come out less well in the highly geared company.

The third year 19–3 is a good year and both companies can meet their interest charges whilst leaving substantial earnings for the ordinary shareholders. Already, the shareholders of Company A show a higher return, 15 per cent, compared to the 11·25 per cent to the shareholders of Company B.

In a good year, the shareholders come out better in the highly geared company.

The fourth year 19–4 is a very good year. The return to shareholders in both companies goes up but the shareholders of Company A are able to secure a return of 35 per cent compared to the 23·7 per cent for Company B's shareholders.

Gearing has a bright side in that it can dramatically increase the earnings of equity in the good years and a dark side in that in the bad years it can drastically reduce the equity earnings.

This is a clear indication of increased risk. By allowing priority claims of fixed returns to some of the capital employed by the company, the equity shareholders take over a greater share of the risks of the undertaking. It follows that high gearing increases risk to equity and whilst companies can easily achieve gearings of up to 30 per cent without this affecting investors' views of the riskiness of the shares, there will be a point beyond this level at which investors begin to look for higher earnings from shares which are highly geared. There are exceptions to this rule, and property companies often achieve very high gearing because of the security of their underlying assets.

Since all companies must bear in mind the need to raise new capital in the future, it follows that a company may be ill-advised to increase its gearing beyond the point where the stock market will need to reappraise the degree of risk of its shares.

A paradoxical effect of high gearing is that the fixed-interest investor will also consider that the chances of his interest being paid in a bad year are reduced. More important, where long-term debt is repayable in fixed terms, the company may not be able to find the cash required when redemption becomes duc.

High gearing, therefore, also increases the risks to lenders and may have the effect of pushing up the rate of interest at which the company may borrow.

These arguments have led some analysts to conclude that there is, ultimately, little advantage in gearing since the average return required for capital, whatever its source, will tend to remain the same. Practical experience, however, seems to indicate that there is a real advantage in companies taking a reasonable proportion of gearing.

The effects of gearing in British industry can be seen from the table below.

The tobacco industry in 1960 showed a basic rate of return or estimated return in capital invested (in Column 3) of 7·9 per cent which compares unfavourably with the rate of 10·2 per cent shown in the metal-goods industry.

RETURN ON INVESTMENT IN BRITISH INDUSTRY 1960

GOING-CONCERN BASIS

	Return to Net Worth (1) %	Proportion of Debt to Total Finance* (2) %	Estimated Return to Capital Invested (3) %
Manufacturing			
Food	10·5	22·7	8·8
Drink	10·6	28·4	8·4
Tobacco	11·2	40·5H	7·9
Chemicals and allied industries	9·9	22·7	8·3
Metal manufacture	11·6	23·6	9·6
Non-electrical engineering	9·5	19·2	8·3
Electrical engineering	7·8	25·5	6·6
Shipbuilding	6·5	16·5	5·9
Vehicles	11·7	22·0	9·8
Metal goods	11·6	16·0L	10·2H
Textiles	8·4	17·6	7·4
Leather and fur	4·1L	37·4	3·7L
Clothing and footwear	12·9	27·2	10·2H
Bricks, pottery, glass and cement	11·0	16·5	9·7
Timber, furniture	10·4	31·4	8·1
Paper, printing and publishing	10·5	26·0	8·7
Other	8·4	30·6	6·7
TOTAL MANUFACTURING	10·1	23·2	8·4
Distribution and Services			
Construction	9·1	31·6	7·2
Transport and communication	9·2	20·6	7·9
Wholesale distribution	8·8	28·6	7·1
Retail distribution	12·1	22·7	10·0
Miscellaneous services	12·8H	29·7	10·0
TOTAL SERVICES	10·7	34·6	8·6
TOTAL ALL INDUSTRY	10·2	23·7	8·5

* Net worth plus total debt (long and short term).

From "Investment Planning by Private Enterprise"—A. S. Ashton (District Bank Review, October, 1962).

However, as can be seen in Column 2—Proportion of debts to total finance—the tobacco industry uses a very high gearing of 40·5 per cent compared to only 16 per cent used by the metal-goods industry. The result is that the return to equity (net worth), shown in Column 1, in tobacco is geared up to 11·2 per cent, which is nearly as good as the return to equity (net worth) in metal goods of 11·6 per cent.

Notice also that the proportion of gearing varies widely from as little as 16 per cent in the metal-goods industry to as high as 40·5 per cent in tobacco.

THE LIMITATIONS OF ACCOUNTING INFORMATION

All that has been said so far about the going-concern or accounting assessment of profitability or return on investment has stressed the uses to which that assessment can be put whilst outlining the problems involved in determining the capital base and the related income.

A number of criticisms of accounting data are often voiced and these warrant examination.

THE COST BASIS OF VALUATION

Assets acquired by a firm are entered in the books at cost and, if still retained by the firm at the end of the year of operation, will be valued in several ways—

Fixed assets are valued at cost less the accumulated depreciation for the current and previous years.

Investments are valued at cost, but a company is required, if the investments have a quoted stock exchange valuation, to state what the market value is at the date of the Balance Sheet.

Stocks are valued at the cost or market value, whichever is lower.

It may be necessary, in assessing the capital in use by a firm, to adjust the accounting figures.

Fixed Assets

Some fixed assets, such as land and buildings, may have depreciated at a slower rate than has been used in the accounting records. In fact, land and buildings may have appreciated rather than depreciated in value: in calculating the capital employed it is perfectly legitimate to amend the values so as to make them realistic.

Other fixed assets such as plant and equipment may have a

greater value than is shown in the books: it may also be that worn-out and obsolete plant has little real current value.

A fair valuation may be the price at which the asset could be sold *less* the cost of removal and disposal. This may be substituted for the book value shown in the Balance Sheet.

Investment

This may, in any case, be removed from the capital base as being idle assets not employed within the business. If the view is taken that they should be included in the capital base, however, they may be valued at current market value, rather than at cost. Since the value of investments is subject to considerable fluctuation, however, it may be preferable to take an average market value over the period.

Stocks and Work-in-progress

The convention of valuation—cost or market value whichever is lower—is, of course, highly conservative. Future losses on stocks are anticipated because current stocks are valued at market price if this is lower than cost. Future profits are not anticipated because a higher market value of stock does not affect the valuation put on a stock, which remain at cost. It seems more consistent, when we are assessing the capital base, to include stocks at current market value, or replacement value.

THE PROVISION FOR DEPRECIATION

The basis on which depreciation is usually calculated has already been outlined. There is in the U.K. no obligation on a company to charge depreciation against profits: nor will depreciation charges correspond to the capital allowances allowed for tax purposes.

It has been suggested that fixed assets should be valued at replacement values—often identical with insurance valuations—and this is, perhaps, the soundest practice to adopt. The replacement value will, of course, allow for the age of the asset by taking the current cost of a new asset and deducting "depreciation" for the years in which it has been in use.

GOODWILL

Goodwill in a Balance Sheet usually represents the difference in price paid for a subsidiary or constituent company over and above the book value of its underlying assets.

It is not a valuation of goodwill in the sense of the value of the present standing of the company. In fact, whereas goodwill would, one assumes, tend to increase in value as a firm establishes its organization and reputation, accounting practice is to eliminate goodwill from the books as soon as possible and it is generally written off against profits within the first few years of its arising in the books.

INFLATION

There can be no doubt that in the post-war years the reporting of company profitability was seriously distorted by the effects of inflation. Some companies have adopted procedures for periodical revaluation of their assets, particularly land and buildings, to bring these in line with current values, but many company Balance Sheets, taken at their face value, give little indication of the real value of their assets. Inevitably, profitability looks healthier than it really is if the figures taken over a long period are not adjusted to a common basis which eliminates the effects of inflation.

In the short run, unless the price level rises sharply, the effect is not so serious.

RESOURCES OMITTED FROM THE BALANCE SHEET

Every firm has resources which have a capital value which does not appear in the Balance Sheet. A professional firm, for instance, employs skilled human resources which are the main source of profitability and formal contracts may be executed to retain those resources within the firm. A calculation of profitability for such a firm, based on the assets shown in the Balance Sheet, has little meaning. As in the case of other intangible assets, it would be possible to make valuation of these resources in terms of the present value of their future earnings for the firm and thus to calculate a meaningful profitability.

Patents and Trade Marks may be shown at cost, which is the cost of the legal fees involved in registering the rights or, perhaps, the price paid in purchasing them. In the former case, there may be no relationship at all to the real value of the right which is difficult to value until serious exploitation has begun. Even then, some patents lose their value very rapidly if new inventions of substitutes are produced so that reliable valuations are hard to come by.

Leased Assets present a particular, and growing, problem. It is possible for a company to acquire most or even all of its assets by leasing arrangements which commit it to continued periodical payments out of income, on a firm contractual basis. The company is using assets and, in fact, creating indebtedness of a long-term nature without this showing in the Balance Sheet. Indeed the nature of the leasing arrangement is that the assets remain the property of the lessor. Because of this, the rights of the providers of long-term funds through debentures or shares may be seriously prejudiced without their being aware of the fact. Equally, reported profits may appear better than they are because residual profits from leasing arrangements inflate reported profits whilst there is no increase in the capital base. Leasing arrangements create hidden gearing and because it is hidden give rise to quite false assessments of risks.

* * *

These limitations in the accounting information need to be recognized and accepted. Properly understood, they may lead to adjustment to the accounting data, which, nevertheless, produce assessments of profitability which are fair and acceptable.

There is no substitute for the accounting systems which produce accurate and reconcilable data about the firm. However, the data is historical and subject to the accounting conventions which are designed to provide conservative statements of profit which all parties interested in a firm can accept as not extravagantly misleading (in the direction of optimism).

Essentially, accounting data is concerned with past performance and with assessing the going-concern. Whilst it has some relevance to the future it can only make a limited contribution to the assessments of future projects.

3 *Management of Funds and Types of Investment Projects*

In the previous chapter we considered the accounting methods of assessing the rate of return on investment as a means of assessing the efficiency of an undertaking as a going-concern. The limitations of the accounting method were pointed out and the fact that we have no substitute for the methods, at present, was also noted. We concluded, on the whole, that accounting methods of assessment of profitability can only be concerned with assessment of past profitability.

STANDPOINT FOR EVALUATION

If we wish to assess the profitability of new projects then we must decide which point of view we are going to take and we must look for other methods than the accounting method to assess the alternatives which face the business firm.

In assessing a new project we must take the standpoint of the managers of the undertaking who stand as the custodians of funds, entrusted to them, in the main, by long-term investors. These long-term investors may be shareholders or debenture holders.

PREDICTIONS

The managers have to make, in the first place, a prediction which will lead to the use of funds. The predictions they make will be concerned with the likely outcome of an investment. They will want to compare the capital invested with the ultimate returns which may be received over the life of a project.

ALTERNATIVES

They will also be concerned with exploring the full range of alternatives that lie before them and of making effective comparisons between these alternatives which will enable them to select the best from the whole range.

RISKS

Managers will also have to assess the risks involved in their predictions and in the estimates on which they base their comparisons of the alternatives. As far as possible they will want to quantify these risks.

PROFITABILITY

In general, the managers will have two ways of calculating profitability, one is known as the internal rate of return and this will be explained in fuller detail later. The other method of calculating profitability is to calculate the present worth of an investment at a given rate of return. Again, a fuller explanation of this method is given later. Before considering these two instances, could afford to ignore a National Plan if it attempted to set targets for growth and development over the whole range of industry.

SOURCES OF INFORMATION

Managers must base their decisions on information. In the main this may come from within the firm, and, if so, it will come from accountants, economists and technical specialists, such as engineers and scientists. Where some alternatives are being considered the firm can expect its existing staff to have the expertise and technological know-how to evaluate the prospects which lie before it. This is not to say that the decision on any alternative can be given entirely by the specialists within the firm. They may be governed, to some extent, by their existing practices and may tend to undervalue new developments as against new exploitation of older developments. If a firm is faced with completely new technologies then it is unlikely that it can from its own resources make an effective valuation of an alternative and, in this case, it may have to bring in consultants from outside.

COMPETITORS

There are many sources of information concerning the alternatives which come from outside the firm. Most firms keep a close watch on the policy and behaviour of direct competitors. If a competitor decides to go for a new type of product, then the firm will certainly make a close investigation to see whether it ought also to be developing in that direction.

MARKET RESEARCH

The firm's own salesmen are also a valuable source of information of new products and competitors appearing on the market and, if properly managed, can be a good source of information about potential needs which the firm might consider attempting to satisfy. Trade associations also often run information services which can give access to contacts from abroad for import and export and which often act as a channel for bringing inventors and patentors into contact with firms who might be willing to exploit their inventions and patents. Certain Government publications also act in this way and the Government also publishes a great deal of statistical information which could indicate the size of market, the rate of growth of the market and the likely developments of markets in the future. No firm, for instance, could afford to ignore a National Plan if it attempted to set targets for growth and development over the whole range of industry.

GOVERNMENT

Government departments, such as the Board of Trade, are also sources of information on demands which arise from industry and from the Government. The Government is itself a major investor and a major customer for many industries.

A consistent scanning of the information available to the firm will show that, in general, firms are not short of alternatives. Managers must establish procedures for making a systematic survey of these alternatives so as to make the best use of the funds which come available to them through the natural course of business and through periodical appeals to the shareholders and debenture holders for new funds.

PRINCIPLES OF EVALUATION

The principles on which projects can be evaluated are simple enough. What is not so simple is the application of these principles in a consistent and thorough-going manner to the data which comes available to managers.

The three basic principles are (*a*) the incremental principle (*b*) the return on investment principle and (*c*) the comparisons of alternatives principle. Let us look at each of these principles in turn.

THE INCREMENTAL PRINCIPLE

The incremental principle simply states that the profitability of a firm can only be changed in so far as its existing commitments can be changed. Given that a firm has a rate of profit and a degree of capital invested for generating that profit then, from the economic point of view, it can only change its profitability by affecting the level of investment or its level of returns. If a new project will not affect the profits being made it can nevertheless increase profitability if it reduces the investment necessary to earn that profit. On this basis a manager who is offered a new machine which is cheaper to use than an old machine may consider buying it even though it does not increase the profits which he will earn. It will increase his profitability if his capital investment is reduced.

If a project will increase the profits which a firm is earning then it may be worthwhile even if it involves an increase in the capital committed.

Changes in profitability can be effected by increasing the returns to a firm, either by means of increasing sales revenue or by lowering costs and either of these alternatives may result in an increase in the overall profitability of the firm.

RETURN ON INVESTMENT PRINCIPLE

The return on investment principle implies that the incremental investment involved in a new project must be associated with the incremental returns. In other words, if we know the amount by which profits can be increased then we can compare this increase to the amount of additional capital which must be employed on the project and if this shows a satisfactory rate of return then the effect of the profit on the firm's profitability will also be satisfactory. If a firm has an existing return of 20 per cent on capital invested and a new project offers a 20 per cent return then we can be sure that the resultant overall rate of return, provided our estimates of the return on the new project are correct, will also be at the rate of 20 per cent.

COMPARISON OF ALTERNATIVES

The principle of comparison of alternatives states that for every possible project there will be an alternative and this alternative will usually offer a different rate of profitability. Of course it is an alternative if a firm decides to do nothing but usually there are alternative actions which offer a firm profitability. A choice must then be made between the different projects. A dynamic and active enterprise should have no shortage of alternatives for capital investment. It is true that some declining industries may be in the situation which offers few alternatives within that industry but, in this case, the enterprise will be faced with the choice of staying within the industry and declining with it or of seeking new outlets and diversifying activities. To say that an enterprise has no alternatives in the use of funds is simply to state that management does not have an active and dynamic approach to the future. Funds for investment are fluid: they can move from one sphere of activity to another. All businesses are concerned with profitability and all managers must ensure that the alternatives they select for the investment of their funds are such that they offer reasonable profitability to the investors providing those funds.

FUTURE COSTS AND PAST COSTS

A few points need to be made in relation to these principles which will become clearer as we go on. The first point is that in discussing future alternatives, only future costs and revenues are relevant. As stated above, where we are considering an increment in investment, only increments of investment and profit need to be considered. In any case, only the future increments are relevant to the decision. "Sunk" or past costs, such as charges for depreciation, are irrelevant to future decisions. In the previous chapter we showed that the charges for depreciation are calculated on certain expectations which if they prove incorrect will result in a loss being charged against profits in a particular year. Such an accounting loss is a book entry. From the point of view of the future such a cost is irrelevant. It should not affect, for instance, the decision as to whether to replace the machine or not. If we are looking at the decision to replace a machine and a book loss is likely to occur, then the loss occurred at the point when the machine was purchased not when the fact became evident three years later! The fact that a wrong decision has been made on a previous machine should not inhibit a manager from making the right decision on a new machine.

In making these statements we are concerned solely with the logic of the decision. This does not say that we would not sympathize with the practicising manager who shrinks from requesting funds for a new machine if this involves admitting that a previous decision to buy a machine was incorrect. Nevertheless there can be no doubt in which direction the logic lies!

A further point which needs to be emphasized in relation to the principles of project evaluation is that the differential costs or incremental costs relating to the particular decision to be made are not necessarily the same as variable or direct costs as these are reported under accounting systems. Each project must be carefully investigated before the costs and profits and capital investments to be associated with it can be identified.

THE PROBLEMS OF CAPITAL BUDGETING

Managers in budgeting for their capital expenditure are faced with a whole series of problems which can be dealt with under four headings: (*a*) the demand for capital, (*b*) the supply of capital, (*c*) the rationing of capital and (*d*) the timing of investments.

THE DEMAND FOR CAPITAL

Every firm which is a going-concern has at its command a whole range of managerial skills, ranging from the skills of the production engineer through to the skills of the salesman and the advertiser and marketing man. It includes the skills of the accountant and the research and development engineer, and those of line and staff managers and of top management. It includes the skills of personnel managers and work study engineers. Although all these members of the staff in an enterprise are charged with day-to-day responsibilities which have been limited in accordance with the organizational structure of the firm, it is normally found that there arises from all of them a demand for an improvement in the performance of the firm. An active top management will encourage these demands and it is therefore inevitable that there should be a flow of requests for capital expenditure. It is necessary in the present day, given the scale of the enterprises that we are running, that all levels of management should be involved in a systematic survey of fresh opportunities whether these opportunities are cost saving or for new investment. There must be a procedure for screening these demands for capital in terms of profitability and this implies that all levels of management must have a good understanding of the criteria of profitability. Unless this understanding is present the firm will find too many projects coming up for approval which have been insufficiently justified in economic terms. It will be found that if the criteria for evaluation in financial terms are understood and are commonly accepted as being rational and scientific, that the decisions which are made on the allocation of capital become much more acceptable at all levels. Failure to accept and establish common criteria for evaluation will result in the all too common situation where the engineers believe that the accountants are against capital expenditure on principle and the accountants believe that the engineers are for spending without regard to profitability, etc.

THE SUPPLY OF CAPITAL

The supply of capital within the firm may come from two main sources.

Internal. The first source is the internal source, the retained cash income which arises from the normal operation of the firm. This retained cash income which is the accounting profit plus any non-cash costs, such as depreciation, is attributable eventually to the normal shareholders after the interest and dividends have been paid to debentures and preference shares. It is incorrect, however, to consider that retained earnings have no cost. Internal funds retained on behalf of ordinary shareholders must be used as profitably as funds obtained by means of share issue.

External. The long-term external sources of funds are the sale of equity shares, the issue of long-term borrowing and preference shares.

There are also many short- and medium-term sources of finance. As was noted in the previous chapter it is possible for a firm to borrow, in effect, by leasing the majority of its assets. Equally, it is possible to obtain hire-purchase terms but this is a fairly expensive way of borrowing money. Banks and other financial institutions will also be prepared to lend money on loan, or on overdraft. Various other sources are available, such as the factoring of debtors. All these sources will have a cost which must be met before there is any reward in a project for the ordinary shareholders. The only exceptions are the trade creditors, the effects of which are offset, to some extent, by the compulsory lending which must be made to trade debtors.

Although the supply of money in the economy fluctuates from time to time, it will, in general, be true that a well-established enterprising firm, which has a profitable record and good opportunities, will have little difficulty in raising capital in one way or another. That capital, however, will have a cost which must be met before there is any increase in the profitability of the firm.

RATIONING OF CAPITAL

The rationing of capital is necessary not so much because capital may not be fully available but because the scale of increase of capital investment of a firm must be kept within certain bounds. Even if top management is prepared to grow from being a £5,000,000 company to being a £500,000,000 company it must establish a rate of growth which will enable its human resources to cope with the problems of organization and change which that growth will imply. At any given moment in time then, a firm will have to place some limits on its capital spending. Top management will be aware of the likely scale of the supply of capital in the coming year. This may be stipulated in fairly broad terms, for instance £5,000,000 or £50,000,000 and it may very well be subject to this sort of change; that £5,000,000 becomes £6,000,000 and £50,000,000 becomes £70,000,000. All levels of management will accept that their ideas on spending must be subject to scrutiny and the rationing system should not establish a strait jacket but a means of effective disciplining of the demand for capital.

Classifying Investment Opportunities

Given that this is the case, it will be necessary for management to establish the various categories of investment opportunities. This is dealt with in more detail below, but it should be noted that not all investment opportunities should, or would, bring the same kind of rate of return. Managements must be clear about the size and scale of these different categories and must establish a rate of return for each category if that be appropriate. A balance must be kept between the various categories and each investment considered must be related to the overall picture of company development. There will have to be a balance between investment, for instance, in research and development as compared to investment in sales promotion or in new systems in the office. In particular years competitive pressures may force the main burden of capital investment to be made in a particular direction. If rapid technological change is taking place in computers, then firms who are marketing computers will have to find the capital to keep abreast of current developments in order to maintain their future product lines. Failure to do this may result in the firms going out of business. This could mean that capital for investment in welfare and sales development projects was in very short supply.

Cut-off Rate

For each category of investment it is also necessary to decide a cut-off rate. This is a minimum rate below which a firm will not consider accepting an investment. If we know that the rate of return we are looking for is a minimum of 10 per cent then we can rank projects in order of rate of return and accept those projects which offer more than 10 per cent. If we have more projects offering more than 10 per cent than we have capital available to exploit them, then, other things being equal, we would accept those projects giving the higher rates of return. Acceptable projects giving more than 10 per cent would have to be deferred until such time as the capital was available, when they would again take their chance in the queue. Projects which offer less than 10 per cent, if this be a long-term rate of return, would not be acceptable and would be definitely rejected.

Balancing Risks

A further problem of rationing would be the evaluation of

the risks in all the projects considered. It would be necessary to establish the right balance of risk and this may decide the projects which are accepted in the current year. If higher rates of return involve higher risks then it may be advisable to have a suitable balance of low-risk projects at or about the cut-off rate with high-risk projects with very high rates of return.

Also involved in capital rationing will be the authorization of those projects which offer no return or which are not susceptible to a profitability analysis. These projects should come last on the list because if they offer no profitability then their acceptance implies that other projects must compensate for this lack of profitability.

TIMING

The timing of investment is important because all capital investment must be related to the general business conditions prevailing at the time of investment. Political, economic and social factors all influence the current climate of opinion which may affect a firm's decision on whether to make investment which offers a suitable profit. The prospect of nationalization of certain fields of activity may persuade a firm that it is better to postpone investment in that field until the situation has been clarified. Capital projects, typically, may take some years to mature and management may be more concerned with the prospect of conditions which will be in existence in a few years' time rather than in reacting simply to the existing climate of opinion. Such factors as whether Great Britain will join the Common Market must affect a decision on whether to build a new processing plant in the U.K.

CATEGORIES OF INVESTMENT PROJECT

A. S. Ashton, the Treasurer of Esso Petroleum Ltd., has established four categories of investment project and these are worth individual consideration.

NO-RETURN PROJECTS

The first category is the no-return project and typical of this is spending on welfare facilities which may be of an optional or an obligatory nature.

Optional no-return

Many firms build sports fields for their employees on the basis that this will have, ultimately, a beneficial effect on the firm's operation, but it is, of course, impossible to put this kind of calculation into £ *s. d.* The investment can certainly be put into money terms but the benefits will be of an extremely indirect and nebulous nature.

Obligatory no-return

Similar types of expenditure must be incurred occasionally by law. Safety measures required by the inspectors of factories and other requirements imposed by the various Factory and Offices Acts are examples of this kind of spending. There is no option and if a firm is to stay in business it must make this kind of expenditure.

MAINTAINING OLD BUSINESS

The next category of investment project is to maintain existing business. Many proposals for capital expenditure will come from a going-concern under this heading. Works and plant managers will propose replacements of assets in order to maintain efficiency within the operating unit. This category of project is the most difficult to evaluate because it may be difficult, if not impossible, to show that any improvement of profitability or reduction of costs will result from the replacement of assets. On the other hand, it may be that if an asset is reaching the end of its life, then a failure would mean that existing profitability was entirely lost. In general, top management will act with restraint in investing in this category. There is a danger, in the long run, that the firm will find itself with a beautifully re-equipped manufacturing unit ready to make products which are no longer in demand.

This is not a new problem as the following extract from a speech by the First Lord of the Admiralty at Portsmouth in 1866 indicates—

> If we must needs keep up an old Fleet, we cannot expect a new one too. We have plenty of ships which would have been very useful in the year 1846. They are now about as useful as postchaises, but we have taken such care of them that we have had little to spare for the substitutes which present times require.
>
> Happy the nation that had no Navy ten years ago! That is what

has sent the Americans so far ahead. Every sixpence of their expenditure has been upon vessels of real and immediate efficiency.

COST REDUCTION

This third category of project is the cost-saving project and this type of scheme is much more susceptible to a profitability analysis. If capital investment results in the reduction of costs, then, other things being equal, that capital investment may be justified. Where cost reduction schemes are associated with systematic engineering approaches such as value analysis and work study, it may very well be that a reasonable proportion of a firm's capital investment should be devoted to this type of investment. Certainly this category would take preference over the previous category which has as its object the maintenance of the existing business as it is.

EXPANSION AND NEW PRODUCTS

The main category of investment projects must be those which involve making new products, improving designs and meeting expansions in demand. These are the real directions in which new profitability can be looked for.

New Products

The most important sub-division is the expansion in the direction of developing new products, processes or services. This is indeed the direction in which Government policy is most anxious to encourage development. It is in applying new ideas and techniques within industry that this country has its best chance of survival in a competitive world.

New Designs

Design is an important factor in the saleability of products, both ergonomically and aesthetically. Good industrial design should not only be applied to consumer goods: all products should be designed for ease of use by the user and for "good looks." In some products such as fashion clothing, design is the essence of the product and a new design *is* a new product.

Expansion of Demand

Because of the heavy costs incurred in developing new products and new production facilities, a firm which caters for rising demand can show substantial cost savings as it expands its production capacity. The result should be a steadily falling price to the customer even whilst profits are improved or maintained.

Expansion, however, may also mean the acquisition of existing businesses and this also may be approved by the Government where it involves a rationalization and a concentration of resources into more effective manufacturing units. Some expansion may involve the purchase of securities by way of trade investments or acquisition of interest in subsidiaries. By themselves these are financial operations which do not involve special considerations and if no changes in manufacture follow upon them then it can be argued that they are not a desirable means of deploying new funds of a manufacturing firm.

SUMMARY

The firm which wishes to appraise future projects must bear in mind the present standing of the company and its long-term plans and development policies; it must make a systematic survey of the available alternatives which are open to it whether these be technological or market or product alternatives; and it must assess these alternatives in economic terms and in terms of the incremental investment and profit which will result from them.

Every firm must establish procedures for supplying and rationing the capital of the firm and must bear in mind the problems of risk and uncertainty and intangibles, all of which will affect its final decision on whether to accept projects or not. It must have a clear conception of the various categories of investment projects which are open to it and ensure that a fair balance is kept between those projects which offer expansion and real opportunities of profitability and those which offer no return but may, nevertheless, find justification. It must remember that the projects offering a return must, in the long run, pay for those projects which do not give a return. As A. S. Ashton says, companies which have a too high proportion of no-return projects, or projects that simply maintain their existing business are "wealthy but doomed."

4 Return on Investment—New Project Evaluation

APPRAISAL of a project involves the comparison of the net cash investment with the net cash returns which that investment will produce.

CASH INVESTMENT AND RETURNS

The net cash investment is the cash required at the start of a project to acquire the fixed assets and to provide the requisite working capital (stocks, debtors, etc.). If old assets are disposed of, the cash proceeds of the sale may be deducted from the cash investment required, so that only the net cash required is taken into calculation.

The net cash returns are the cash earnings from sales of the product or service less the cash payments for running costs (labour, materials, cash expenses, etc.). Depreciation and other "book charges" such as provisions are *not* cash payments and are therefore not deducted. Tax on profits, however, *is* a cash payment and should be deducted from returns at the time when the tax payment is made.

If the fixed and working capital have a cash realization value at the end of the life of the project, this can be treated as a net cash return.

As an example of the net cash investment let us take a case where the project involves the purchase of fixed assets costing £10,000 and there will be working capital required by way of stock, debtors, etc. of £2,000. The asset is to replace an old asset which can be disposed of for £500 cash.

NET CASH INVESTMENT

	£
Cost of fixed assets	10,000
less Proceeds of old asset replaced	500
	9,500
Working capital required	2,000
Net cash investment at Time 0	£11,500

Irrespective of book value of the old asset the calculation of the net cash investment will be as shown.

If the cash returns on this project are cash sales, £20,000, against which are offset costs on a normal accounting basis of £15,000 and the costs include non-cash charges of £3,000 and if the average rate of tax is 50 per cent then the calculation of the net cash returns will be as follows—

NET CASH RETURNS

		£
Sales, annual		20,000
less Costs	15,000	
Non-cash charges	3,000	
		12,000
		8,000
Taxable profit £5,000 (Sales less Costs)		
Tax at 50%		2,500
Net annual cash return (Years 1–10)		£5,500

A complete picture of the project can be built up if we can also specify the result of the sale of the assets at the end of its life. Let us assume that the project has a life of ten years and the proceeds of sale of assets will be as follows—

	£
Proceeds of sale of fixed assets Year 10	1,000
Proceeds of disinvestment of working capital Year 10	2,000

This information can be brought together in a simple way if we deal logically with the time scale. Let us adopt a convention that the investment will take place in Time 0 and that subsequent returns will therefore occur at the end of Year 1, Year 2, etc. The information can then be presented in the way shown below.

		Investment £	Returns £
Time 0	Net cash investment	11,500	
Year 1	Cash returns		5,500
Year 2	Cash returns		5,500
Year 3	Cash returns		5,500
Year 4	Cash returns		5,500
Year 5	Cash returns		5,500
Year 6	Cash returns		5,500
Year 7	Cash returns		5,500
Year 8	Cash returns		5,500
Year 9	Cash returns		5,500
Year 10	Cash returns		5,500
Year 10	Additional cash returns from capital disinvestment		3,000
	TOTALS	£11,500	£58,000

This presentation shows us in simple form what are the total investments involved, £11,500, and what are the total returns involved, £58,000. Presenting the information over the whole life of the project in this way poses for us a simple question. What is the rate of return on this project?

Before we go on to answer this question let us look at the various ways which have been proposed to assess how far the project is worth while. After all, we are only interested in profitability if this gives us a good guide as to whether to back the project or not.

A number of methods of dealing with this problem have been suggested, some of which have a limited value, some of which are of very little value indeed. These are considered in turn.

COMPARATIVE COSTS

The first method often used in assessing whether to undertake a project or not is comparative cost. Let us take a simple example and assume that the decision whether to undertake a project is to be based on the initial cash outlays.

We have three projects as follows—

	PROJECTS		
	A	B	C
	£	£	£
Net cash investment	50,000	50,000	50,000

On the basis of the initial cash outlay of £50,000 it would not be possible to discriminate between the three projects. Any one of them would be equally acceptable or equally unacceptable. Clearly, this is not a very satisfactory way of approaching the decision on whether to undertake a project. Comparative cost does have a very limited use, however, in so far as the initial cash outlay on a project may indicate the scale of the project and therefore whether it is likely to fall within the acceptable range or not. If, for instance, the three projects A, B, and C were houses for personal occupation, then for most people the size of the investment would be beyond their means. If, on the other hand, they are small factories, then many small businesses could contemplate spending that amount of money. Comparative initial cash outlay, then, can be useful in indicating the scale of the project and whether it is worth while making a more detailed evaluation. The inadequacy of the comparative cost measure of the attractiveness of these three projects can be seen if we assume the following pattern of cash returns to be associated with the three initial cash outlays—

		PROJECT A £	PROJECT B £	PROJECT C £
Time 0	Initial cash outlay	50,000	50,000	50,000
Year 1	Cash returns	25,000	25,000	20,000
Year 2	Cash returns	25,000	25,000	20,000
Year 3	Cash returns	—	25,000	20,000
Year 4	Cash returns	—	—	25,000
	TOTAL CASH RETURNS	50,000	75,000	85,000

It can be seen that the three projects offer quite different cash returns. Project C offers £85,000 returns for the £50,000 investment as compared to the mere £50,000 which would be returned if Project A were accepted. Clearly, comparative initial cost is of no value in determining profitability.

PAY-BACK OR PAY-OUT PERIOD

The next method of evaluation is the pay-back or pay-out period of the project.

The pay-back or pay-out is the length of time required for the cash returns from a project to equal the total initial cash outlay.

If the cash returns from the project are at an annual uniform rate then the pay back can be calculated as follows—

$$\frac{\text{Cash outlay}}{\text{Annual cash returns}} = \text{pay-back period in years}$$

For instance, if a project involves a cash outlay of £50,000 and there are uniform annual returns of £25,000 then the calculation is—

$$£\,\frac{50{,}000}{25{,}000} = 2 \text{ years pay-back period}$$

This is the pay-back period for Projects A and B above. The same calculation shows that the pay-back period for Project C is $2\frac{1}{2}$ years.

If the cash returns are not uniform, that is they differ each year, then it is necessary to find the period by means of trial and error. The cash returns for each successive year are taken until the total equals the initial cash outlay. For instance, if a project involves a capital outlay of £50,000 and the returns in the first year are £15,000, in Year 2 £20,000, in Year 3 £30,000, in Year 4 £40,000, it can be seen that the total pay-back at the end of Year 2 is £35,000. The additional pay-back in Year 3 is £30,000 which is in excess of the initial capital outlay so that the pay-back must be between two and three years. If the £30,000 is assumed to arise at a uniform rate throughout the year, we can assume that the £15,000 required to give complete pay-back would occur half way through Year 3 and the pay-back period would therefore be 2½ years.

Returning to our example we see that Projects A and B both give a more favourable pay-back than Project C, since in these two cases the capital of the project is recovered at the end of two years. However, it is clear that pay-back is not a satisfactory appraisal of profitability since Project C not merely pays back the capital in the first 2½ years but would also pay back an additional £25,000 in Year 4 and £15,000 in Year 3. Furthermore, although Project C shows a less favourable pay-back, of 2½ years, it offers greater returns over its four year life than do projects A and B. It must be assumed, incidentally, that Project A will cease to give any returns at the end of Year 2 and Project B will cease to give returns at the end of Year 3 although the capital remains tied up for four years.

The value of pay-back, however, does not lie in assessing profitability, but in assessing the *riskiness* of a project. It is clear that Project C is riskier than Projects A and B since it will take a longer time for it to pay back the £50,000 cash invested in it.

THE PAY-OUT PLOT

The usefulness of the pay-back (or pay-out period) in assessing the period over which the capital invested in a project is expected to be at risk is such that most systems of capital investment appraisal will include the calculation.

Its usefulness can be increased by the use of the pay-out plot which is simply a graphical presentation of the cumulative cash returns on a project expressed as a percentage of the original capital investment.

By expressing the returns as a percentage of the original

investment, it is possible to compare the riskiness of projects of different sizes. By plotting the cumulative returns, it is possible to show, not merely the point at which the capital is fully returned, but also the intermediate points at which various proportions of the capital outlay will have been returned. Figure 4/1 shows the pay-out plot for two Projects A and B.

The cash investments and returns are as follows—

		A	B
		£	£
Time 0	Cash investment	20,000	100,000
Year 1		8,000	20,000
Year 2		8,000	20,000
Year 3		4,000	60,000
Year 4		2,000	20,000
Year 5		6,000	Nil

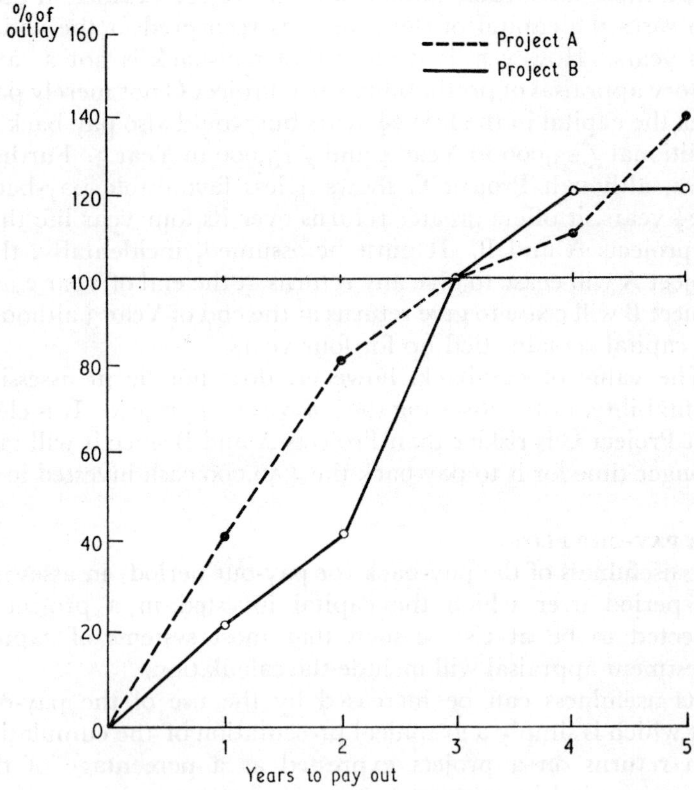

Figure 4/1. PAY-OUT PLOT

The graph brings out clearly the fact that, although the two projects have the same pay-out period, Project A brings quicker returns within that period.

If the plot is extended beyond the pay-out point (100%), the illustration also shows that at the end of five years, Project A will have produced higher returns, as a percentage of capital outlay, than Project B. In other words, the pay-out does not assess profitability.

AVERAGE RATE OF RETURN ON INVESTMENT (BEFORE TAX)

A commonly used method of assessing the profitability of a project is the accounting method: that is a method which assesses the accounting profit as a percentage of the original cash outlay.

In this method, the average annual net profit, after depreciation and cash outlays have been deducted from sales revenues, is expressed as a percentage of the original cash outlay.

This method involves three calculations—

1. Calculate the annual rate of depreciation by taking the investment in fixed assets less the expected residual value. This gives the total depreciation expected and this is charged annually over the life of the assets.

2. Calculate the average annual profit after deduction of depreciation, operating costs and expenses.

3. The average rate of return is then—

$$\frac{\text{Average annual profit}}{\text{Net cash investment}} \times 100 = \text{per cent return}$$

Applying this calculation to the previous example, we find the results are as shown at the top of page 50.

This method clearly discriminates to a greater extent than pay-out between the three projects. It shows a greater profitibility for Projects C and B and also shows Project A to have a zero profitability.

Less satisfactory variations of this approach usually take profitability over the first year or so of a project's life. This is a satisfactory procedure only if the cash returns are likely to be

		PROJECT A	PROJECT B	PROJECT C
		£	£	£
Time 0	Net cash investment	50,000	50,000	50,000
Year 1	Cash returns	25,000	25,000	20,000
Year 2		25,000	25,000	20,000
Year 3		—	25,000	20,000
Year 4		—	—	25,000
		50,000	75,000	85,000
	Life	2 years	3 years	4 years

Straight-line Depreciation (assuming no residual value of net cash investment)

	PROJECT A	PROJECT B	PROJECT C
$\frac{\text{Capital cost}}{\text{Life}}$ = rate per annum	£25,000 p.a.	£16,666 p.a.	£12,500 p.a.
Average annual profit before tax	Nil	£8,334	£7,500 for 3 yrs. £12,500 for 1 yr. £8,750 p.a. average
Average rate of return	0%	16%	17·5%

uniform. Also, the depreciation rate is vital, since it incorporates the estimate of the life of the project.

The danger, however, lies in adopting depreciation rates which consider only the technical life of the fixed assets, rather than estimating the potential duration of the project which may be determined by market factors and technological obsolescence. These may indicate a radically different project life.

A further danger lies in ignoring taxation. Since capital expenditures may attract favourable allowances according to the type and location of the assets acquired, it is essential to take tax into account. This point is dealt with in greater detail later.

The main criticism of this approach, however, is that it does not adequately take into account the timing of the cash returns.

This point can be illustrated by the example below—

		PROJECT F	PROJECT G	PROJECT H
		£	£	£
Time 0	Net cash investment (100% depreciable)	3,790	3,790	3,790
Year 1	Cash returns	1,500	1,000	500
Year 2	Cash returns	1,250	1,000	750
Year 3	Cash returns	1,000	1,000	1,000
Year 4	Cash returns	750	1,000	1,250
Year 5	Cash returns	500	1,000	1,500
		5,000	5,000	5,000
Net average annual cash returns		£1,000	£1,000	£1,000
less annual depreciation (20% per annum)		758	758	758
Average annual net profit		£242	£242	£242
Initial investment		£3,790	£3,790	£3,790
Average rate of return on initial investment		6·4%	6·4%	6·4%

By working on an average basis over the whole life of the three projects, we find that an average rate of return of 6·4 per cent is shown for each project.

Yet a closer examination of the pattern of cash returns shows a radical difference between Project F and Project H. Of course, calculation of the pay-out will give the answer to the question: which project would the manager prefer? Does not Project F offer earlier returns and therefore less risk? But cannot we also say that Project F offers greater profitability, too? We will return to this point later.

It should be noted in relation to this method that the average rate of return may be calculated on the basis of the average investment involved in the project. If £3,790 is paid out initially and recovered at a uniform rate over the five years, then the *average* capital employed is 50 per cent of £3,790, or £1,895.

On this basis, the return on all the projects above would be doubled, i.e. £242 profit on £1,895 average capital employed = 12·8 per cent.

NET PROFIT TO INVESTMENT RATIO

A method of evaluation similar to the average rate of return is the net profit to investment ratio.

This calculates the ratio between the total cash returns after deducting all outflows (including current costs and capital costs) over the whole life of the project and the net cash investment. An example is shown below—

		PROJECT D	PROJECT E
		£	£
Time 0	Net cash investment	50,000	50,000
Year 1	Cash returns	40,000	20,000
Year 2	Cash returns	10,000	30,000
Year 3	Cash returns	40,000	25,000
Year 4	Cash returns	10,000	25,000
		£100,000	£100,000

The net profit on Projects D and E is £50,000 (£10,000–£50,000) so that the net profit to investment ratio is in each case 1 : 1.

This approach is of little value since the "net profit" is not related in any way to the period of time over which it is earned. Clearly a 1 : 1 ratio obtained over four years would be more satisfactory than the same return obtained over six years. It is also less satisfactory than a 1 : 1 return over two years.

REQUIREMENT FOR A SATISFACTORY METHOD

The average rate of return is the more useful of these aproaches since it expresses the return as an annual rate and, to that extent, takes into account the total duration of the project.

What has been said so far in criticism of the methods of project evaluation proposed indicates the requirements which a satisfactory method must meet.

Firstly, it must be based on a forecast covering the whole life of the project and expressing the investment and the returns in cash terms.

Secondly, it must provide a method of evaluating the different profitabilities of projects, such as F and H above, which have similar lives but give dissimilar patterns of cash returns.

Such a method can be found if we realize that money has a time value. This is a familiar notion, indeed a fact of life with which we are all well acquainted. Yet it has powerful implications if it is applied consistently to project appraisal.

THE TIME VALUE OF MONEY

To illustrate the idea that money has a time value, let us take a simple case of a simple man, Robinson, who has an article for sale. Let us say that he is selling bungholes (whatever they may be, and whatever use people may make of them).

Robinson is approached by Green, who wishes to buy a bunghole, and after some haggling, they agree on a price of £1, which Green pays on the spot.

Robinson is then approached by Brown, who is also able to find a use for bungholes and agrees to buy one from Robinson for £1. As Robinson is wrapping the bunghole up, however, Brown, with some diffidence, explains that he cannot pay spot cash for the goods, and he asks Robinson if he can pay in one year's time.

Robinson, whilst simple, is not *too* simple and he reasons

along these lines: "Green has paid me £1 now, but Brown wants to pay me in a year's time. Surely, I should charge some interest? If I put Green's £1 in the bank now, it will be worth £1 1s. in a year's time if the bank pay 5% interest." He therefore suggests to Brown that, if he, the seller, waits for a year, then Brown, the buyer, should pay a larger sum. This should be at least £1 1s.

A person lending money will charge interest.

Now let us make different assumptions. In this case, Robinson is approached first by Brown, who buys a bunghole for £1 and asks for one year's credit. Robinson is simple enough to agree, so that Brown is paying £1 in a year's time.

Green follows Brown in this case, and buys a bunghole from Robinson. When he comes to pay, he says to Robinson: "You have just sold a bunghole to Brown for £1 in a year's time. I will pay you 19s. 1d. now because if you put it in the bank at 5 per cent, it will accumulate to £1 by the end of the year." Since he is no worse off, Robinson should accept.

By his action, Robinson recognizes that the *present value* of £1 received in a year's time is 19s. 1d., if the interest rate is 5 per cent.

So long as money can earn interest, so long will it be true that the value of £1 received in the future will be worth less than £1 received today.

If we know the rate of interest (or profit), then it is possible to put a present value on £1 received in the future.

THE PRINCIPLE OF EQUIVALENCE

Irrespective of the actual times when moneys are received, sums received or paid out at different times can be brought into equivalence provided we know the rate of interest (or profit).

1. Let us take an example and assume that no one pays interest on money: money does not have a time value. If this is so then—

£100 at Time 0 (now) = £100 at Year 1 = £100 at Year 2 and so on.

2. Now let us assume that money has a time value and it will earn 10 per cent interest if invested. If we have £100 in hand today, then—

£100 at Time 0 = £100 + £10 at Year 1 = £110 + £11 at Year 2.

10 per cent time value: £100 now = £110 in one year = £121 in two years.

This is the compound interest principle.

3. Assuming that money has a time value of 10 per cent, what must be invested now to accumulate to £100 in two years' time?

We can work backwards:

£100 at the end of Year 2 is equivalent to—

$$£100-\left(\frac{10}{110}\times 100\right)=£91 \text{ at the end of Year 1}$$

£91 at the end of Year 1 is equivalent to—

$$£91-\left(91\times\frac{10}{110}\right)=£83 \text{ at present (beginning of Year 1)}$$

This is the discounting principle. Discounting is reciprocal of the interest.

For project evaluation, tables of discount factors are available and these can be found at the end of the book.

USE OF TABLES A AND B

Table A shows the present value of £1 received at a future time (1–50 years) at a stipulated discount rate (1 per cent to 40 per cent).

For example, £1 received in two years at 10 per cent has a present value of £0·826. £1,000 received in two years at 10 per cent has a present value of £826.

Table B is a cumulative form of Table A. It shows the present value of an even flow of £1s received annually over a period (1–50 years) at a stipulated discount rate.

Example £1 received for three years at 10 per cent.

	Table A	Table B
Year 1	£0·909	£0·909
Year 2	0·826	1·726 (sum of 1 and 2)
Year 3	0·751	2·487 (sum of 1, 2 and 3)

If £1,000 per year is received for three years at 10 per cent, then this has a present value of £2,487.

USE OF TABLE A

Using Table A, we shall find that differing amounts received at different times can be compared. For instance, we may ask: is it better to receive £1,500 in two years' time or £3,000 in six years' time?

If the interest rate is 10 per cent, then Table A gives the factor which expresses both these sums in equivalent terms of present worth.

	10% Factor	Present Worth
£1,500 in 2 years	0·826	£1,239
£3,000 in 6 years	0·565	£1,695

The later receipt of £3,000 offers greater present worth.

If the interest rate is 20 per cent, which is better?

	20% Factor	Present Worth
£1,500 in 2 years	0·694	£1,041
£3,000 in 6 years	0·335	£1,005

Under these circumstances it is better to take £1,500 in two years' time: the rate of interest is so high as to give the later receipt of £3,000 a lower present value.

This simple example of the effect of the rate of interest on the value of money paid or received in the future can be seen graphically below.

Graphical Presentation

The present value of £1 at up to thirty years has been plotted at various discount rates. The graph can, of course, be used instead of Table A.

A significant point is the relatively slow decline of present value at the lowest discount rate 5 per cent. In contrast, present value declines sharply with the high discount rates. It follows that the choice of the rate of discount may be important in project evaluation. Moreover, the higher the discount rate, the shorter the length of time over which accurate forecasts of future receipts or payments is necessary. If a 25 per cent rate is taken, then receipts after fifteen years will be of little value—less than £·05 per £1. Looking at this in another way, we see that a project involves substantial receipts at the end of, say, thirty years; the present value of these receipts will not be very different even if the rate is 15 per cent rather than 25 per cent. In the earlier years, however, the

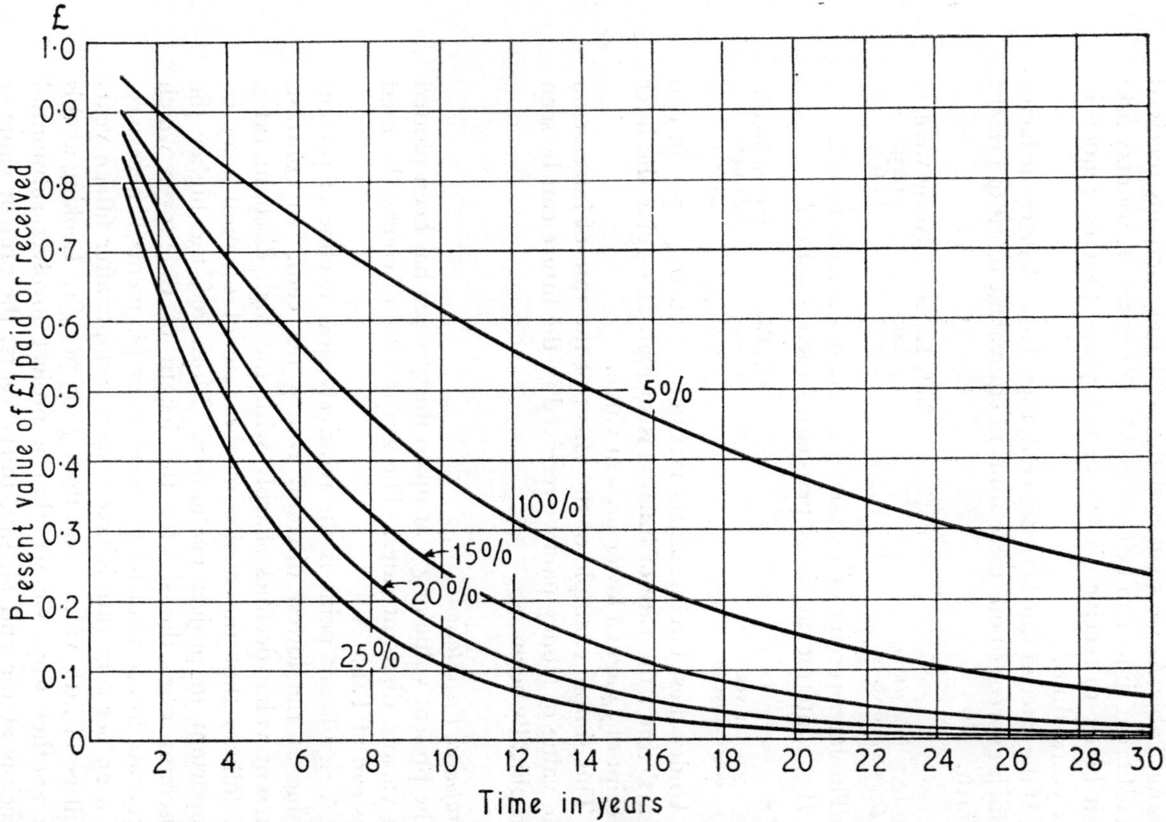

Figure 4/2. PRESENT WORTH OF £1 PAID OR RECEIVED DISCOUNTED AT 5, 10, 15 20, AND 25 PER CENT

difference in rate is significant. At seven years, the value of £1 at 15 per cent is almost twice the value of £1 at 25 per cent.

USE OF TABLE B

Table B can be used whenever a stipulated sum is to be paid or received annually over a period of years. Where the life of a project is known, it is simply a more convenient aid to calculation.

It has another use, however, which involves the calculation of a factor.

The factor is obtained by dividing the net cash investment by the annual cash returns. This gives the factor.

Using the factor we can calculate the life a project must have if a given rate of return is to be obtained. Alternatively, if the life is known we can calculate what the rate of return is.

The procedure is—

If *the life of the project* is known scan Table B horizontally along the life row until the factor is found. The column in which it is found indicates the discount rate or rate of return.

If *the discount rate* is known scan down the column on Table B until the factor is found. The row in which the factor stands indicates the life which the project must have.

Example

An investment of £3,000 can earn £750 per year.

$$\text{The factor is } £\frac{3{,}000}{750} = 4{\cdot}0.$$

1. If the project has a life of five years, scanning Table B at the five-year row shows that the factor at 8 per cent is 3·993 and at 6 per cent it is 4·100. The rate of return is therefore a little below 8 per cent.

2. If the project must earn at least 15 per cent, scanning the 15 per cent column of Table B shows that the factor at six years is 3·784 and at seven years 4·160. The project must have a life of nearly seven years if it is to return 15 per cent.

DISCOUNTING CONVENTIONS

In project evaluation, compound interest is used, and there are several conventions which may be adopted. The most common are—

1. *Annual Compounding*. In this convention it is assumed that all sums are received as a single lump sum at the end of the year.

2. *Monthly Compounding*. This assumes that the receipts are obtained in twelve equal monthly annual instalments.

3. *Annual Compounding* (middle of year receipt). This method is similar to the first since it is assumed that a lump sum is received at annual intervals. In order to compensate for the fact that receipts may, in actuality, flow in continuously over the year, the factors are calculated on the assumption of mid-year instead of year-end receipt.

4. *Continuous Compounding*. This assumes that there is continuous receipt of cash.

Tables are available for all these conventions, but the tables included in this book are annual compounding. These assume that all receipts are received as a lump sum at the end of each year.

Each convention will give slightly different factors, as can be seen if the mid-year and year-end factors are compared.

MID YEAR AND YEAR END COMPARED DISCOUNT FACTORS ON BASIS OF 5% INTEREST PER ANNUM COMPOUNDED ANNUALLY

YEAR I	(*a*) MID YEAR LUMP SUM II	(*b*) YEAR END LUMP SUM VI
1	0·97590	0·95238
2	0·92943	0·90703
3	0·88517	0·86384
4	0·84302	0·82270
5	0·80288	0·78353

It is generally recognized, however, that since evaluation of projects is based on estimates rather than definite knowledge of the future, it is unnecessary to seek excessive precision: factors calculated to three places of decimals are quite accurate enough and the choice of compounding convention is not vital.

These differences are important to the financier who is making calculations of the cost of money or the price to be charged for its use.

In project evaluation, however, we assume that a firm is considering alternatives and is using the discount factors to place these on a comparable basis. Basically, it is asking "will a project pay?" The choice of discounting convention is unlikely to affect the answer.

METHODS OF USING DISCOUNTED CASH FLOW

There are three main ways in which the formula for discounting may be applied to capital expenditure decisions.

1. The net present-value method.
2. The yield method. (Also called the rate of return, internal rate of return, profitability index, marginal efficiency of capital etc.)
3. The annual-value method.

It is generally agreed that the net present-value method is the best, although, properly used, all the methods should give the same selection of investment projects.

Where projects do not have uniform annual cash returns and where there is a strong element of risk and uncertainty, the net present value and yield method are most suitable.

Where projects do have uniform cash flows and there is little risk and uncertainty (as in the case of public utilities) then the annual value method may be more suitable.

The method of applying each method to the evaluation of a project will now be shown by means of examples.

There are also two other methods which use the mathematics of discounting but are not strictly discounting criteria. These are—

4. The terminal-value calculation.
5. The annual capital charge. This method is used by some nationalized industries and a few commercial companies.

The tables can also be used for—

6. Sinking fund calculations.

NET PRESENT VALUE

The present value of a project is found by discounting all future cash flows at a stipulated discount rate. If the sum of these *exceeds* the initial outflow, then the project is giving a higher return than the evaluation rate.

Let us take examples of projects in a company which requires a minimum rate of return of 8 per cent.

Reference to Table A shows that the discount factors at 8 per cent are—

Year 1	0·926
Year 2	0·857
Year 3	0·794
Year 4	0·735

PROJECT A		£	8% Factor	Net Present Value
				£
Time 0	Net cash investment £50,000			
Year 1	Cash returns	25,000	0·926	23,150
Year 2	Cash returns	25,000	0·857	21,450
	Present value of cash returns at 8%			£44,600

Since the net cash investment, £50,000, exceeds the net present value of the returns from this project, £44,600, the project does not return 8 per cent. The project does not meet our requirements.

PROJECT B		£	8% Factor	Net Present Value
				£
Time 0	Net cash investment £50,000			
Year 1	Cash returns	25,000	0·926	23,150
Year 2	Cash returns	25,000	0·857	21,450
Year 3	Cash returns	25,000	0·794	19,850
				£64,450

By contrast to Project A, this project brings in returns of £64,450 net present value at 8 per cent. Since these exceed the investment of £50,000 required, the rate of return is well above 8 per cent. This project meets our requirements easily.

PROJECT C		£	8%	Net Present Value
				£
Time 0	Net cash investment £50,000			
Year 1	Cash returns	20,000	0·926	18,520
Year 2	Cash returns	20,000	0·857	17,140
Year 3	Cash returns	20,000	0·794	15,880
Year 4	Cash returns	25,000	0·735	18,380
				£69,920

Again, Project C meets our requirements more than adequately since it produces returns having a present value at 8 per cent of £69,920 in return for an investment of £50,000.

YIELD

By trial and error, all future cash flows from a project are discounted at a series of discount rates until the rate is found at which the present value of outlays and returns are equal. This is the internal rate of return, or yield.

As an example, let us look more closely at Project C. What is the yield or internal rate of return?

Trial 1. Has already been made at 8 per cent—

			Present Value at 8% P.V.
		£	£
Time 0	Net cash investment £50,000		
Year 1	Cash returns	20,000	18,520
Year 2	Cash returns	20,000	17,140
Year 3	Cash returns	20,000	15,880
Year 4	Cash returns	25,000	18,380
			£69,920

Since the net present value of the returns exceeds the net cash investment, the rate of discounting is too low. Another trial is necessary.

Trial 2. Guessing, let us double the discount rate to 16 per cent.

This gives the following results—

			Present Value at 16% P.V.
		£	£
Year 1	Cash returns	20,000	17,240
Year 2	Cash returns	20,000	14,860
Year 3	Cash returns	20,000	12,820
Year 4	Cash returns	25,000	11,040
			£55,960

The net present value of the returns still exceeds the net cash investment. The project rate of return is, therefore, above 16 per cent.

Trial 3. Guessing again, let us take a 20 per cent discount rate. This gives the following result—

			Present Value at 20%
			P.V.
		£	£
Year 1	Cash returns	20,000	16,660
Year 2	Cash returns	20,000	13,880
Year 3	Cash returns	20,000	11,580
Year 4	Cash returns	25,000	9,640
			£51,760

This is very near, but the discount rate is still too low. Another trial is necessary.

Trial 4. The next rate in the table is taken, since the result is quite close.

			Present Value at 22%
			P.V.
		£	£
Year 1	Cash returns	20,000	16,400
Year 2	Cash returns	20,000	13,440
Year 3	Cash returns	20,000	11,020
Year 4	Cash returns	25,000	9,020
			£49,880

This shows that 22 per cent is too high a discount rate since the net present value of the returns is less than the net cash investment.

It is clear therefore, that the rate of return lies somewhere between 20 per cent and 22 per cent.

Approximate Interpolation

Since intermediate discount rates are not given in the table, a fairly accurate calculation of the rate of return can be obtained by using the following method—

$$\frac{\text{Net cash investment less lowest present value}}{\text{Highest net present value less lowest net present value}} \times \text{Difference between discount rates}$$

this is—

$$\frac{£50{,}000 - 49{,}880}{£51{,}760 - 49{,}880} \times 2 = \frac{120}{1{,}880} \times 2 = 0{\cdot}127$$

The yield or internal rate of return is therefore 22 per cent less 0·127 or 21·873 per cent.

Graphical Interpolation of the Yield

A graphical method of reducing the number of trials required in calculating the yield is sometimes used. This method is used in connexion with the profitability ratio. The procedure is as follows—

Step 1. Several trials of discount rates are made. At least two trials must be made and the present values calculated.

Step 2. A profitability ratio for each trial is calculated—

$$\frac{\text{Net present value of outlays}}{\text{Net present value of returns}} = \text{Profitability ratio}$$

Step 3. The yield or rate of return is the rate at which the profitability ratio equals 1. This is found by graphical interpolation.

To illustrate this process, let us take an example of a project which has a life of four years. In the first place, the firm will pay out £2,000 in initial capital investment. This will be followed a year later by a further investment of £3,000. After that, cash returns will be received of £1,000 at the end of the second year, £3,000 at the end of the third year and £4,000 at the end of the fourth year.

In the calculation of the present values, below, the data has been arranged so that the zero point of the project is the time at which investment has been completed. Consequently, the initial investment of £2,000 is considered as taking place at zero minus one year. The present value factor is, therefore, more than 1. At an evaluation rate of 10 per cent, the £2,000 investment has a present value of £2,200. At 20 per cent it would have a value of £2,400.

			Factor	Net Present Value	
		£		£	£
Year 1	Net cash investment 2,000		1·1	2,200	
Time 0	Net cash investment 3,000		1·0	3,000	
Year 1	Cash returns	1,000	0·909		909
Year 2	Cash returns	3,000	0·826		2,478
Year 3	Cash returns	4,000	0·751		3,004
				£5,200	£6,391

and this gives a profitability index of—

$$\frac{5{,}200}{6{,}391} = 0{\cdot}817$$

At 20 per cent, the ratio is—

$$\frac{5{,}400}{5{,}231} = 0{\cdot}625$$

The internal rate of return can be calculated by plotting these values on a graph as in Fig. 4/3.

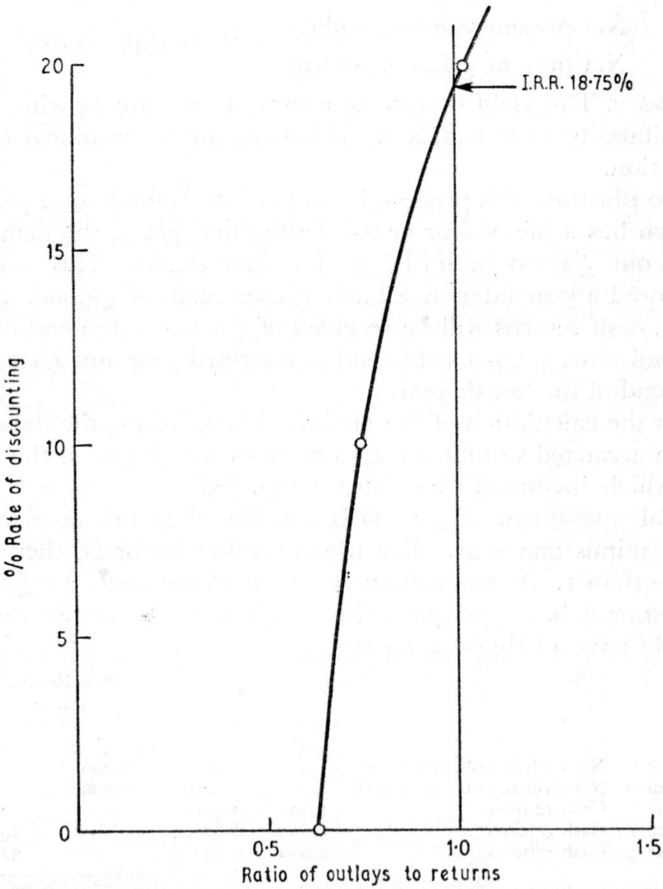

Figure 4/3. PROFITABILITY RATIO INTERPOLATION CHART

On the vertical axis is shown the rate of discounting taken.

On the horizontal axis is shown the ratio between the outlays and the returns.

The ratio at each discount rate taken is plotted and the points connected by a line. A vertical line is drawn where the profitability index is 1·0.

The point at which the two lines intersect is the yield or internal rate of return.

With practice, it is often found that a good guess at the rate of return can be obtained and the yield method is not so tedious as might be thought. This does depend however on the variability of the pattern of cash flows.

Comparison of Rates of Return

Let us look back at the examples of projects which we took. How does the yield or internal rate of return compare with the other rates calculated?

On page 46 Projects B and C showed—

		PROJECT B	PROJECT C
		£	£
Time 0	Net cash investment £50,000		
Year 1	Cash returns	25,000	20,000
Year 2	Cash returns	25,000	20,000
Year 3	Cash returns	25,000	20,000
Year 4	Cash returns		25,000
The average rate of return was calculated as		16%	17·5%
In contrast to this the yield of the two projects is		just over 22%	just under 22%

On page 50 Projects F, G and H showed cash flows of—

		PROJECT F	PROJECT G	PROJECT H
		£	£	£
Time 0	Net cash investment (100% depreciable)	3,790	3,790	3,790
Year 1	Cash inflow	1,500	1,000	500
Year 2	Cash inflow	1,250	1,000	750
Year 3	Cash inflow	1,000	1,000	1,000
Year 4	Cash inflow	750	1,000	1,250
Year 5	Cash inflow	500	1,000	1,500
		£5,000	£5,000	£5,000

and the average rate of return on the initial investment was 6·4 per cent for each project.

The yield or internal rate of return of each project is—

F	G	H
13% approx.	10%	9% approx.

This shows the way in which the internal rate of return discriminates between, for instance, projects F and H, giving greater weight to the fact that project F gives larger returns at the beginning of the project.

Projects D and E on page 51 showed the following pattern of returns and outlays—

		PROJECT D	PROJECT E
		£	£
Time 0	Net cash investment	50,000	50,000
Year 1	Cash returns	40,000	20,000
Year 2	Cash returns	10,000	30,000
Year 3	Cash returns	40,000	25,000
Year 4	Cash returns	10,000	25,000
		£100,000	£100,000

The net profit to investment ratio was in each case 1 : 1.

Was this a sound assessment of their relative profitabilities?

If the discounted cash flow principles are used, the yield of the two projects is shown to be different. Project D returns about 40 per cent (just a little more). Project D returns about 32 per cent or 33 per cent. Again, the method takes into account the differing cash flows which are more advantageous in Project D.

THE ANNUAL-VALUE METHOD

All expenditures are converted to equivalent annual costs by the use of discount tables and capital recovery factors. It is assumed that only costs are significant for the decision and the costs include both depreciation and interest on capital.

The annual capital charge may be compared with the net cash flow and if there is an excess annual cash flow then the project is acceptable.

This method is used by property companies and public utilities because it is most useful, technically, when a firm—

(*a*) is largely financed by fixed interest capital,

(*b*) has stable costs and revenues,

(*c*) is not liable to obsolescence.

It can be used by companies to which these conditions do not apply but it then becomes more cumbersome than the net present value and yield methods.

The procedure to be followed is—

(*a*) The costs of the alternatives over their respective lives are expressed in terms of net present worth.

(*b*) These are converted to equivalent annual expenditures by use of the capital recovery factors given in Table C.

Let us take an example of a firm faced with a problem whether to buy a new machine for £2,000 or to buy a second-hand machine for £1,000. The new machine will have a life of five years and associated annual running and maintenance costs of £200 for two years, rising to £210 for two years and £220 in the final year.

The second-hand machine has a life of three years and will cost £500 per annum to run and maintain.

The relative cash flows, which are all outgoings, are as follows—

		Buy New Machine	Buy Second-hand
		£	£
Time 0	Total initial outlay	2,000	1,000
Year 1	Maintenance, repairs and running costs	200	500
Year 2		200	500
Year 3		210	500
Year 4		210	—
Year 5		220	—
	Life	5 years	3 years

Let us assume, once again, that the company looks for a minimum rate of return on projects of this nature of 8 per cent.

The first step is to convert the outgoings to their net present value at 8 per cent.

	P.V. Factors	New	Second-hand
		£	£
Time 0	1.000	2,000	1,000
Year 1	0.926	185	463
Year 2	0.857	171	428
Year 3	0.794	166	397
Year 4	0.735	154	—
Year 5	0.681	150	—
NET PRESENT VALUE		£2,826	£2,288

These can be expressed as equivalent annual costs by multiplying the net present value shown above by the capital recovery factors at 8 per cent for the lives given. The factors are given in Table C at the end of the book.

CONVERSION TO EQUIVALENT EXPENDITURES

	New	Second-hand
Capital recovery factor at 8%		
3 year life		0.388
5 year life	0·2505	
Equivalent annual cost	£2,826 × 0·2505 = £708	£2,288 × 0·388 = £888

The comparison shows that the second-hand machine will cost £180 per annum more than the new machine.

PRESENT VALUE OR FUTURE WORTHS?

One approach to project evaluation which is *not* in general use is the calculation of the future worth.

This approach is based on the argument that what a business is interested in is the amount of the investment compared to the future worth of the receipts from a project. If the future worths of the receipts at a stipulated interest rate exceed the amount of the investment, then it might be argued that the project should be accepted.

This approach would measure the profitability of investing a sum of money for a stated period of time. All proceeds are re-invested at the stipulated investment rate. To make the calculation, annual receipts are multiplied by a factor giving their future worth at the end of the project.

A firm is considering a project which involves initial cash outlays of £2,000 and will return £400 per year for four years, followed by £200 in the final year. Since the total returns are £1,800 compared to an outlay of £2,000 the project does not, on the face of it, look a profitable one.

The future worth calculation is—

				Future Worth Factors at 10%	Future Worths
		£	£		£
Time 0	Total outlays	2,000			
Year 1	Returns		400	1·464	585
Year 2			400	1·331	532
Year 3			400	1·210	284
Year 4			400	1·100	440
Year 5			200	1·000	200
		£2,000	£1,800		£2,041

With this approach the receipts are valued in relation to the final receipt. At the terminal date, the receipts are valued at £1 per £1 received. Earlier receipts are multiplied by the factor which is the compound interest rate. In our example, therefore, the receipts in Year 4 are valued at 1+10 per cent = 1·1; receipts in Year 3 are valued at 1·1+10 per cent = 1·21 and so on, working backwards.

The method therefore involves measuring the amount to which the receipts will have accumulated if they are invested on receipt at 10 per cent. It is sometimes argued that since, in the example taken, the future worth of the receipts is equal to the investment, the project returns 10 per cent. This is incorrect.

A feature of the method is the remarkable effect which a small amount received in later years of a project can have. For example—

		Future Worth Factors at 10%	Future Worths at end of 7 years
	£		£
Time 0 Total outlays £2,000			
Year 1	400	1·772	708
Year 2	400	1·611	644
Time 3	400	1·464	585
Year 4	400	1·331	532
Year 5	200	1·210	242
Year 6	2	1·100	2
Year 7	2	1·000	2
	£1,804		£2,715

An increase of £4 in the receipts has increased the future worth of thc project by £674.

The more correct comparison would be to multiply the original investment by the future worth factor also. This would show, in the first case—

	Future Worth Factor at 10%	Future Worth
Time 0 Total outlays £2,000	1·61	£3,220

This may be compared with the future worth of the returns—

	£
Future worth of investment	2,320
Future worth of returns	2,041
Loss of future worth	£1,179

In the second case it would show—

		Future Worth Factor at 10%	Future Worth
Time 0	Total outlays £2,000	1·949	£3,898

Comparing this with the future worth of the returns—

	£
Future worth of investment	3,898
Future worth of returns	2,715
Loss of future worth	£1,183

The two evaluations are identical, since the difference of £4 between the losses of future worth is the difference in revenues between the two projects.

The second method, then, is a valid measure of the firm's situation and, as such, it has its advocates.

Let us compare the results with the yield given in an earlier example, Project B.

The present worth calculation is—

		£	Future Worth Factor at 22%	Future Worth £
Time 0	Net cash outlays £50,000		1·821	91,000
Year 1	Cash returns . .	25,000	1·49	37,210
Year 2	Cash returns . .	25,000	1·22	30,000
Year 3	Cash returns . .	25,000	1·0	25,000

The future worth of the outlays is £91,000 compared to the future worth of receipts of £92,710.

This gives the same result as the yield method—a return of a little over 22 per cent.

The general practice, however, is to use present value calculations rather than future worths.

ACCOUNTING CALCULATION OF PROFITABILITY

If the yield on a discounted cash flow basis is an accurate measure of the true yield of a project and the cash outflows and returns have been correctly estimated, will the accounting reports of a company show the same rate of profitability, assuming that the results of that project are reported over its life? The answer is generally, no.

In most cases the accounting calculation will overstate the yield but the error will not be constant. The precise error will depend upon the length of life of the project, the rate at which depreciation is charged, the asset base used in the calculation, and the extent of the delay between outlays on a project and the returns.

The accounting profitability does not reflect the true underlying yield of a firm or an industry, nor does it provide a consistent ranking.

5 *Techniques in the Application of Discounted Cash Flow Methods*

ONE problem in using discounting techniques is the sensitivity of the evaluation to the discount rate that is chosen. This problem can be handled graphically by the use of the net present value profit (N.P.V.) and cost profiles.

NET PRESENT VALUE PROFIT PROFILE

The N.P.V. profile is obtained by calculating the net present value of a project at various rates of discount. From this is deducted the original cost outlay and the difference is the net present value profit. Its value will be positive if the discount rate is below the internal rate of return and negative if it is above.

Project M involves a net cash investment of £200,000 and will produce returns of £40,000 for ten years. Using the factors from Table B, the N.P.V. profits can be calculated as follows—

PROJECT M

Rate	Factor	×	Cash Flow	=	N.P.V. Returns	−	Original Outlay	=	N.P.V. Profit
			£		£		£		£
0%	10·000	×	40,000	=	400,000	−	200,000	=	200,000
2%	8·983	×	40,000	=	359,320	−	200,000	=	159,320
4%	8·111	×	40,000	=	324,440	−	200,000	=	124,440
6%	7·360	×	40,000	=	294,400	−	200,000	=	94,400
8%	6·710	×	40,000	=	268,400	−	200,000	=	68,400
10%	6·145	×	40,000	=	245,800	−	200,000	=	45,800
15%	5·019	×	40,000	=	200,760	−	200,000	=	760
20%	4·192	×	40,000	=	167,680	−	200,000	=	−32,320

This information is plotted on the chart in Fig. 5/1 and it can be seen that the internal rate of return is a little above 15 per cent.

A comparison of two projects can be made, using the chart.

	PROJECT N	PROJECT O
Cash investment	£200,000	£200,000
Annual net cash returns . .	£460,000	£98,000
Life of project	20 years	5 years
Yield (internal rate of return) .	30%	40%

Judged solely by the discounted rate of return, Project O appears to be the most attractive. However, when the present value profiles of both these projects are compared, the correct choice is not so obvious.

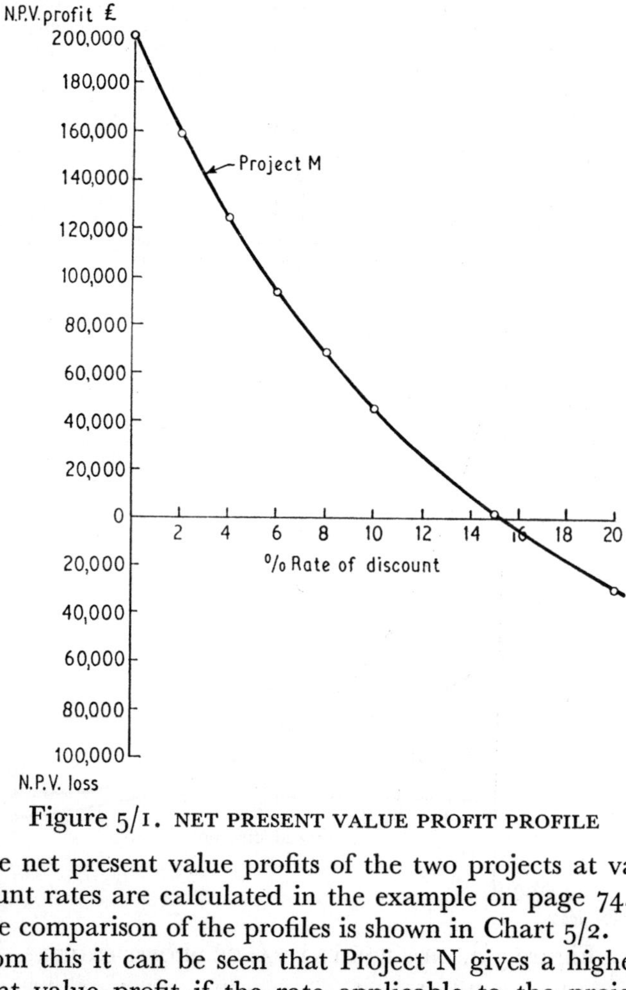

Figure 5/1. NET PRESENT VALUE PROFIT PROFILE

The net present value profits of the two projects at various discount rates are calculated in the example on page 74.

The comparison of the profiles is shown in Chart 5/2.

From this it can be seen that Project N gives a higher net present value profit if the rate applicable to the projects is below 20 per cent. Above that rate, Project O shows slightly higher N.P.V. profits.

Here we need to remember that the predictions of cash returns are, at best, merely estimates. They may be as accurate

PROJECT N

Rate	Factor	×	Cash Flow	=	N.P.V. Returns	—	Outlay	=	N.P.V. Profit
			£		£		£		£
0%	20·000	×	60,000	=	1,200,000	—	200,000	=	1,000,000
4%	13·590	×	60,000	=	815,400	—	200,000	=	615,400
8%	9·818	×	60,000	=	589,080	—	200,000	=	389,080
10%	8·514	×	60,000	=	510,840	—	200,000	=	310,840
20%	4·870	×	60,000	=	292,200	—	200,000	=	92,200
40%	2·497	×	60,000	=	149,820	—	200,000	=	−50,180

PROJECT O

Rate	Factor	×	Cash Flow	=	N.P.V. Returns	—	Outlay	=	N.P.V. Profit
0%	5·000	×	98,000	=	490,000	—	200,000	=	290,000
4%	4·452	×	98,000	=	436,296	—	200,000	=	236,296
8%	2·993	×	98,000	=	391,314	—	200,000	=	191,314
10%	3·791	×	98,000	=	371,518	—	200,000	=	171,518
20%	2·991	×	98,000	=	293,118	—	200,000	=	93,118
40%	2·035	×	98,000	=	199,430	—	200,000	=	−570

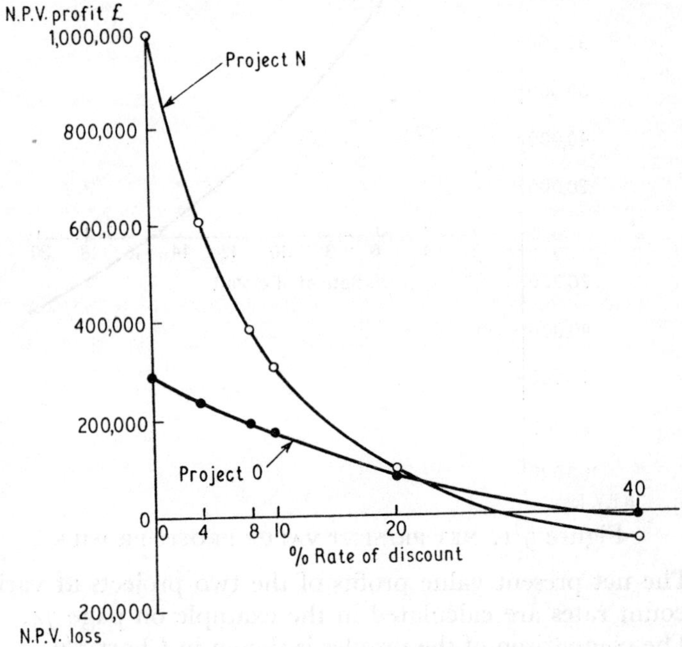

Figure 5/2. NET PRESENT VALUE PROFIT PROFILE

as humanly possible but they are still unlikely to be exactly right. We can say, in fact, that they are more likely to be wrong!

We accept this fact because in any event some forecast or prediction of results must be made if a rational decision on projects is to be obtained.

We can incorporate our estimates of the risks involved in each project on the chart if we first guess the limits within which the cash receipts are likely to fluctuate.

Let us say that the receipts from Project N are likely to fluctuate 5 per cent either side of the first estimate but that Project O is less certain and receipts could fluctuate 15 per cent either side.

The data we have now is—

	PROJECT N	PROJECT O
Cash investment	£200,000	£200,000
Annual cash returns	£57,000–63,000	£83,000–112,700

Each extreme of the range of receipts from each project must be discounted at various rates.

PROJECT N

		N.P.V. RETURNS			N.P.V. PROFITS	
Rate	Factor	High 63,000	Low 57,000	Minus Outlay £200,000	High	Low
0%	20·000	1,260,000	1,140,000		1,060,000	940,000
4%	13·590	855,000	775,000		655,000	575,000
8%	9·818	615,000	555,000		415,000	355,000
10%	8·514	535,000	485,000		335,000	285,000
20%	4·870	306,000	277,000		106,000	77,000
40%	2·497	154,000	139,000		−46,000	−61,000

PROJECT O

		High £112,700	Low £83,300			
0%	5·000	562,500	416,500		362,500	216,500
4%	4·452	502,500	374,000		302,500	174,000
8%	3·993	450,000	333,000		250,000	133,000
10%	3·791	427,000	315,500		227,000	115,500
20%	2·991	337,000	249,000		137,000	49,000
40%	2·035	229,500	169,500		29,500	−30,500

These values have been plotted on the chart in Fig. 5/3.

The shaded area indicates the extent of uncertainties about the projects. The high estimates for Project O will make it preferable either to estimate for N at any discount rate above 17 per cent and preferable to the low estimate for N at 14 per cent and above.

On the other hand, the low estimate for O makes it unfavourable to Project N at all rates shown on the chart.

Project N is the safest.

NET PRESENT VALUE COST PROFILE

This is a graphical presentation of the present value of costs at

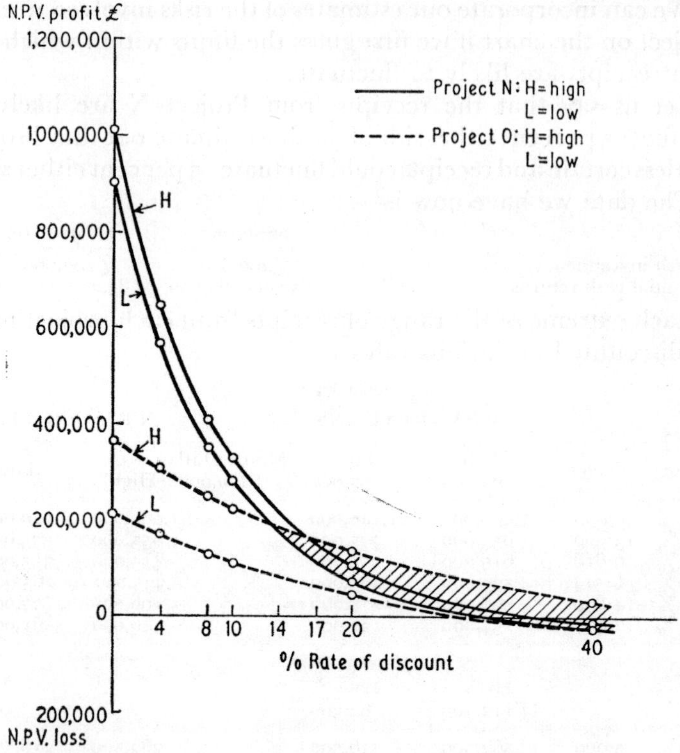

Figure 5/3. NET PRESENT VALUE PROFIT PROFILE

various discount rates, along the same lines as the net present value *profit* profile.

The N.P.V. of the costs of two projects can be plotted against a range of discount rates to give a similar comparison of "cross-over points" and sensitivity of the costs.

The costs of Project A are as follows—

NEW PLANT A

P.V. at Various Rates

	COSTS	2%	P.V.	4%	P.V.	6%	P.V.	8%	P.V.	10%	P.V.	15%	P.V.
	£		£		£		£		£		£		£
Time 0	2,000		2,000		2,000		2,000		2,000		2,000		2,000
Year 1	200	0·980	196	0·962	192	0·943	188	0·926	185	0·909	180	0·870	174
Year 2	200	·961	192	·925	185	·890	178	·857	171	·826	165	·756	151
Year 3	210	·942	197	·889	186	·840	176	·794	165	·751	157	·658	137
Year 4	210	·924	193	·855	179	·792	165	·735	154	·683	142	·572	119
Year 5	220	·906	198	·822	180	·747	163	·681	150	·621	136	·497	109
			£2,976		£2,922		£2,870		£2,825		£2,780		£2,690

Project B shows the following outlays and returns—

NEW PLANT B

P.V. at Various Rates

	COSTS	2% P.V.	4% P.V.	6% P.V.	8% P.V.	10% P.V.	15% P.V.
	£	£	£	£	£	£	£
Time 0	800	800	800	800	800	800	800
Year 1	500	490	481	471	463	450	435
Year 2	500	480	467	445	428	413	378
Year 3	500	471	445	420	397	375	329
Year 4	500	462	427	396	367	341	286
Year 5	500	453	411	373	340	310	248
		£3,156	£3,026	£2,905	£2,795	£2,689	£2,476

These facts are plotted on the Chart in Fig. 5/4 and show that Plant A has lower costs if the discount rate is below 7 per cent. Above that rate, Plant B has lower costs.

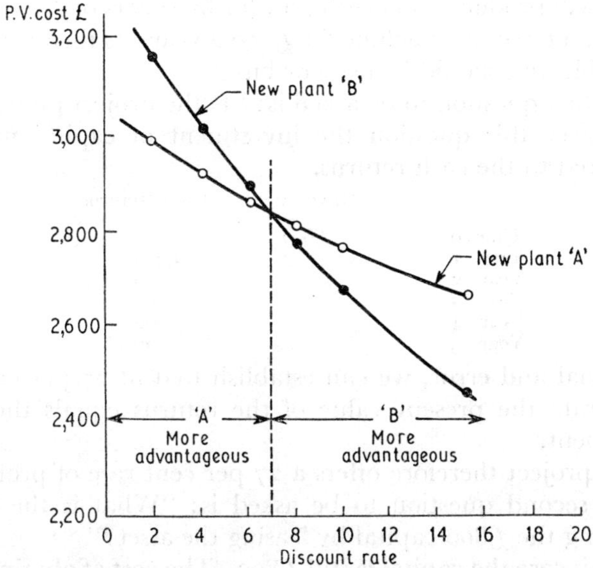

Figure 5/4. PRESENT VALUE COST PROFILE

If a range of estimates for each project is obtained, the N.P.V. cost profiles can be plotted in a similar way to the N.P.V. profit profile in Fig. 5/3 to show the area of doubt and the sensitivity.

HOW TO MAKE APPRAISALS

Since alternatives are not always simple and straightforward, a number of problems arise in making comparisons. Essentially, these are conceptual and there is often a right and a wrong way of approaching the problem.

LEASE OR BUY?

Lease arrangements are, from the financial point of view, merely another way of raising funds. To this extent they are similar to hire-purchase arrangements but the ownership of the asset never passes to the user.

The correct approach to evaluation of level terms may be illustrated by example.

Problem

A business man is considering buying a machine costing £800 which will produce a net cash flow for five years of £300 a year.

He can lease the machine for £250 a year. Is the proposition profitable and should he lease or buy?

The first question to be asked is: "Is the project profitable?" To answer this question the investment of capital must be compared to the cash returns.

	Investment	Cash Returns
Time 0	£800	–
Year 1		£300
Year 2		300
Year 3		300
Year 4		300
Year 5		300

By trial and error, we can establish that at 27 per cent discount rate the present value of the returns equals the £800 investment.

The project therefore offers a 27 per cent rate of profit.

The second question to be asked is: "What is the cost of obtaining the £800 capital by leasing the asset?"

In this case the capital is still £800. The cost of obtaining the use of that capital is £250 per annum.

COST OF LEASING CAPITAL

	Investment	Cost of Borrowing
Time 0	£800	£
Year 1		250
Year 2		250
Year 3		250
Year 4		250
Year 5		250

Again, by trial and error, we can establish that the cost is 20 per cent. This is the rate at which the present value of the lease payments equals the £800 capital borrowed.

Entering into a lease arrangement saves the business man using his own capital. Hence the cost of obtaining £800 in this case is £250 per annum.

Whether this is acceptable depends upon whether it is possible to borrow from other sources, such as a bank, at a lower rate. If it is, then lease finance would be too expensive.

If it is not possible to borrow and the business man has no capital of his own, leasing may offer a way into business. Assuming he wants to go into business, this is saying that he has no alternative way of financing himself.

The following (incorrect) comparison may be made—

	Lease Payments	Cash Returns	Net Cash Returns
Time 0	–	–	–
Year 1	250	300	50
Year 2	250	300	50
Year 3	250	300	50
Year 4	250	300	50
Year 5	250	300	50

Since £50 per year for five years can be obtained for no capital outlay, it would appear that the return is infinite!

In fact, this analysis shows the return to equity (i.e. capital risked by the proprietors of the business). It reflects the degree of gearing as well as the basic profitability. Since high gearing is also high risk, it should not be used as the criterion of profitability of projects.

In fact, the business man is contracted to the lease payments which total £1,250 over the five years. If the returns do not materialize, the payments must still be made.

In most cases, a lease must be initiated by a cash payment and the equity then appears (incorrectly) to be the first instalment. If this arrangement applied to the above project the cash flow would be—

	Lease Payments	Cash Returns	Net Cash Outlays	Net Cash Returns
	£	£	£	£
Time 0	250	–	250	–
Year 1	250	300		50
Year 2	250	300		50
Year 3	250	300		50
Year 4	250	300		50
Year 5	–	300		300

Again, it must be remembered that the real equity risk is the total lease payments to which the firm is contracted. This is the capital which is risked.

AUTHORIZATION OF LEASE ARRANGEMENTS

All lease arrangements should be treated as capital expenditure and the decision on such arrangements made at that level of management at which the decision on outright purchase would be made.

It is incorrect to relate the authorization level to the monthly or annual lease payments or to regard leasing as revenue spending.

HIRE PURCHASE, BUY OR LEASE?

Hire-purchase facilities can be appraised in a similar way to leases. If the Government requires one quarter of the capital sum to be paid as a deposit and the balance over two years, the hire-purchase firm will make the following calculation—

Cash price	£800
less deposit	200
Outstanding	600
Interest 10% for 2 years	120
Amount payable	£720
in two instalments of	£360

The cost of hire-purchase capital is—

	Investment	Cash Costs	Net Investment	Cash Costs
Time 0	800	200	600	
Year 1		360		360
Year 2		360		360

The cost of the capital borrowed is about 12 per cent.

In this case, the deposit represents the equity element in the arrangement.

	H.P. Payments	Cash Returns	Outlays	Net Cash Returns
Time 0	200	–	200	–
Year 1	360	300	60	–
Year 2	360	300	60	–
Year 3	–	300	–	300
Year 4	–	300	–	300
Year 5	–	300	–	300

The rate of return can be found by using the profitability ratio graph (Fig. 5/5) and this shows a yield of 35 per cent. Again, this illustrates the gearing up of equity return due to borrowing which is below the earning rate of the project. It is, of course, associated with greater risk.

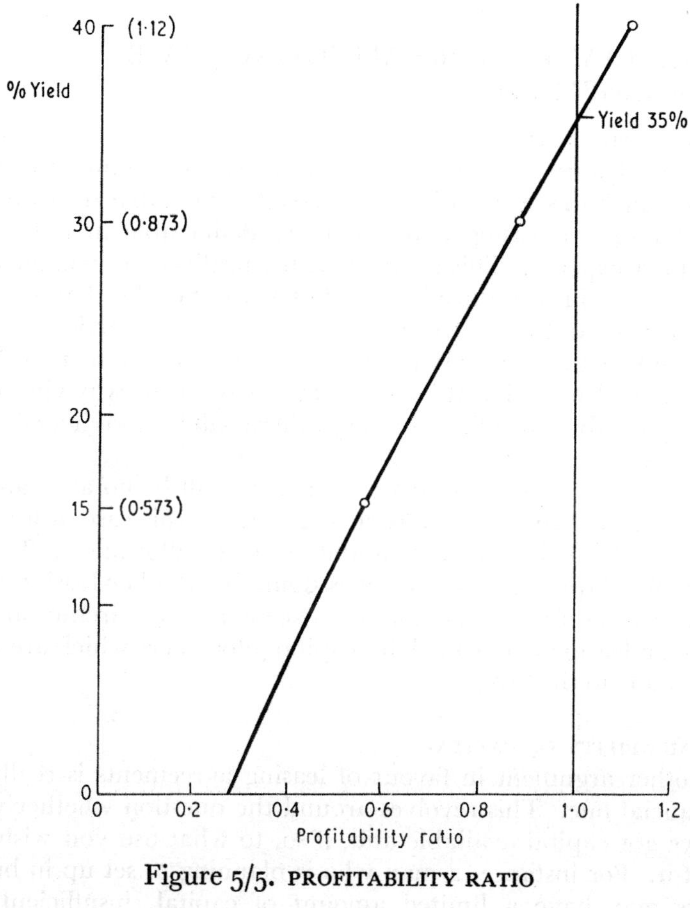

Figure 5/5. PROFITABILITY RATIO

VALUE OF OWNERSHIP ASSETS

A significant difference between hire purchase and leasing is that at the end of a lease the asset remains the property of the lessor.

Appraisal of the hire-purchase arrangement should, therefore, take into account the disposal value of the asset at the end of the project life. If, in our example, the asset is worth £50 at the end of Year 5 then the returns in that year will be £350, not £300. This increase also applies, of course, if the asset is purchased outright and the return of the project is correspondingly increased.

FINANCIAL FACTORS AFFECTING LEASE ARRANGEMENTS

TAX CONSIDERATIONS

Some advantages claimed for leasing revolve round the tax situation of the firm. It is quite correctly stated that the charges paid under a leasing agreement are deductable in full as a business expense. This means that the profits of a firm, for tax purposes, will be reduced by the full amount of the charge paid for leasing and there will be a corresponding reduction in the amount of tax paid. If the leasing charge is £100, then the profits will be reduced by £100 and if the firm is paying tax at an effective rate of 10s. in the £, there will be a saving of £50 on tax.

Of course, this is not to say that there will be no allowances made if the firm buys an asset outright. In this case, a firm is able to claim the relevant capital grants or allowances. These vary from time to time, but it is doubtful whether leasing can offer substantial tax advantages except in rare circumstances when a leasing firm can claim capital allowances which are not available to the firm.

AVAILABILITY OF CAPITAL

Another argument in favour of leasing agreements is really a financial one. This revolves around the question whether you have got capital available and, if so, to what use you wish to put it. For instance, a man who is planning to set up in business may have a limited amount of capital, insufficient to provide both fixed assets and working capital for expenses during the period before he is able to get his business on a full profitable basis. In this case a leasing arrangement may enable him to get into business earlier than would otherwise be the case, and such an individual is not likely to worry too much if the cost of leasing even exceeded the cost of ownership.

In fact, we can say that here leasing offers a possibility which would not otherwise exist. This situation is really like that of an ordinary man who enters into a hire-purchase agreement. The fact that he is able to enjoy the benefit of an asset whilst he is buying it, may be regarded as an incentive for hiring it, because if he were forced to save and sacrifice before he was able to obtain it, he might, in fact, never bring himself to make the effort.

NON-FINANCIAL FACTORS IN LEASING ARRANGEMENTS

PRIDE OF OWNERSHIP

An intangible, but powerful, factor is pride of ownership. Many people and firms have an inherent bias towards owning their assets rather than leasing them. Such firms may not be influenced by arguments showing that leasing is advantageous in some circumstances.

ADMINISTRATIVE COSTS

Another consideration is more important for the larger firms, who must keep records of equipment and who may save on administrative costs if they lease.

DESIGN AND CONSULTANCY

Many lease firms provide a "package deal" whereby they design the layout and provide all the furniture and fittings required, for instance in an executive suite.

QUASI-FINANCIAL CONSIDERATIONS

There are two arguments in favour of leasing, neither of which would find favour with a company accountant and which should be rejected.

The first is that leasing arrangements can be made so that payments come under revenue budgets, thus avoiding the need for authorization under more formal capital budgeting procedures.

The second is that leasing arrangements do not show on the balance sheet of a company, and, therefore, do not affect its credit standing.

The first argument indicates a need for a positive lead from the management accountant. Underlying this is an assumption that capital budgeting procedures are too slow, too cumbersome and, perhaps, too conservative. Capital budgeting should be looking for profitability.

The second indicates a defect in our company law. There is a growing realization that companies should be obliged to disclose the extent to which they are acquiring assets under leasing arrangements in fairness to shareholders and creditors.

PROJECTS WITH DISSIMILAR LIVES

Problem

Two projects, R and T, involve outlays of £4,000 and will bring returns, in the case of R, of £1,900 per annum for three years and in the case of T, £651 for ten years.

The comparison shows—

	R		T		Difference (T-R)	
	Outlays	Returns	Outlays	Returns	Outlays	Returns
	£	£	£	£	£	£
Time 0	4,000		4,000			
Year 1		1,900		651	−1,249	
Year 2		1.900		651	−1,249	
Year 3		1,900		651	−1,249	
Year 4				651		651
Year 5				651		651
Year 6				651		651
Year 7				651		651
Year 8				651		651
Year 9				651		651
Year 10				651		651

The rate of return of Project R is 20 per cent compared to a 10 per cent return on Project T.

The problem is this: Is 20 per cent for three years better than 10 per cent for ten years? The choice of T would mean a loss of £1,249 per annum for three years and this may be looked on as an additional investment which yields £651 from Year 4 onwards. This extra investment yields 4 per cent.

The problem of which project to go for may be handled by estimating what other projects may be available at Year 4 if Project R is undertaken. If the £4,000 funds are re-invested at 2½ per cent at the beginning of Year 4, they will produce

£100 per annum returns. It can now be seen that *in comparison to Project T*, Project R *will show increased cash returns.* The cash flows would be—

		Returns
Time 0	Outlays £4,000	£
Year 1		1,900
Year 2		1,900
Year 3		1,900
Year 4		100
Year 5		100
Year 6		100
Year 7		100
Year 8		100
Year 9		100
Year 10		100

The rate of return to R is, of course, reduced to the weighted average of the two rates (20 per cent for three years and 1·7 per cent for seven years). There will be a point at which the benefit of a high return in early years will be offset by low returns in later years. Long life will not always compensate for lower profitability but it may, sometimes.

The situation is different, of course, where the project with the longer life also shows a higher yield. In this case, estimates of the likely returns to the re-committed funds must be made so as to bring the comparisons to the same life span.

An alternative approach to the problem is to estimate the cash proceeds which would accrue at the end of Year 3 if Project T is terminated. Suppose these to be £2,500, then the pattern of cash flows is—

	Outlays	Returns
Time 0	£4,000	£
Year 1		651
Year 2		651
Year 3		3,151

This represents a rate of return of about 4%. It is lower than the overall rate because the capital recovery is insufficient. (Even on a straight-line depreciation basis, the book value would be £2,800.) On a D.C.F. basis the capital recovery at 10 per cent should be approximately £3,170 at the end of Year 3.

The return on the rest of the life of the project from Years 3 to 10 must be correspondingly higher since the overall rate of return was 10%. If we take the cash flows from Year 3 to 10 to be—

	Outlays	Returns
Time 0	£2,500	£
Year 1		651
Year 2		651
Year 3		651
Year 4		651
Year 5		651
Year 6		651
Year 7		651

The returns on this part of the project are more than 16 per cent.

THE PROFITABILITY INDEX

A convenient and elegant way of ranking projects is the profitability index.

On page 63 the profitability ratio was used as a short-cut to finding the yield of a project with uneven cash flows.

The profitability index is essentially the same relationship except that the formula is—

$$\frac{\text{Net present value of returns}}{\text{Net present value of outlays}}$$

It can be used to show the best choice between projects with differing lives or differing earnings.

Problem

Two projects J and K both involve the investment of £2,000. J will return £2,400 at the end of the first year: K will return £600 per year for five years.

Calculation of the rate of return shows that J yields 20 per cent whilst K yields 15 per cent. Is J necessarily preferred? Only if the company can earn a similar high return for the following four years.

If we assume a required earnings rate of 10 per cent, the profitability index of the two projects is—

$$\text{Project J} \qquad £\frac{2{,}182}{2{,}000} = 1{\cdot}09$$

$$\text{Project K} \qquad £\frac{2{,}274}{2{,}000} = 1{\cdot}14$$

Project K is superior if the company can only invest the

capital released by Project J at the end of the first year at 10 per cent or less.

If the capital released can be re-invested at a higher rate, then calculation of the profitability index at that rate will indicate the relative superiority of that project with the higher index.

PROJECTS WITH DISSIMILAR INVESTMENTS

Many businesses face the problem of how much to spend on initial outlays when it is known that by spending more the cash returns can be increased. The question is, can the additional outlays be justified? In building a hotel or restaurant or running an airline, this is often the case. The life of the projects is the same and they are mutually exclusive. We may do one of the things but not both.

In this case the additional outlays must earn sufficient additional income.

Problem

A hotelier is adding a restaurant to a motel. If he spends £20,000, he estimates that his cash revenues will be £8,500 per annum for three years. If he spends more on décor and facilities he can attract a better class trade. In this case, if he spends £26,000 he will get returns of £11,560 per annum for three years.

The facts may be shown as follows—

	Alternatives 1		Alternatives 2		Difference	
	Outlays	Returns	Outlays	Returns	Outlays	Returns
Time 0	20,000		26,000		6,000	
Year 1		9,500		11,800		2,300
Year 2		9,500		11,800		2,300
Year 3		9,500		11,800		2,300

This analysis confirms the wisdom of using the rate of return of the projects in choosing between them: it is clear that the first alternative is preferable, since it offers 20 per cent. The second alternative offers 17 per cent which is the weighted average of the 20 per cent and 7 per cent returns.

The analysis is useful, however, in that it shows the low

profitability of the increment, which might be compared with other alternatives which could use £6,000. If they offer less than 7 per cent, then alternative 2 might be chosen. Such alternatives include investment outside the business and leaving the money on deposit at the bank.

MULTIPLE-INVESTMENT PROJECTS

A problem arises when projects involve capital expenditure in more than one year.

For example, the statement of cash flows might show—

	Outlays	Returns
		£
Time 0	2,000	
Year 1		800
Year 2		800
Year 3		800
Year 4	1,600	800
Year 5		1,200
Year 6		1,200
Year 7		1,200
Year 8		1,200

Further information is needed before this project can be evaluated. There are several possibilities.

First, is the investment of £1,600 in Year 5 optional or compulsory? If it is optional, then we have two possibilities. The first is that the second investment is added to and modifies the first which would, however, run the full term if we choose not to make the second. In this case we must establish what the cash flows after Year 5 will be if we choose not to make the second investment.

If the result is—

	Initial		Secondary	
	Outlays	Returns	Outlays	Returns
	£	£	£	£
Time 0	2,000			
Year 1		800		
Year 2		800		
Year 3		800		
Year 4		800	1,600 (start of Year 5)	
Year 5		700		500
Year 6		700		500
Year 7		700		500
Year 8		700		500

The implication is that the second outlay prevents revenues from falling and also gives them a considerable boost.

The profitability of each project can be separately evaluated. The initial project offers between 30 per cent and 35 per cent and the secondary project about 9 per cent.

The second possibility is that the second investment is sequential in that no revenues will be received after Year 4 if the additional investment is not made. We then have two projects with a four year life.

The proposition is therefore—

	Initial		Secondary	
	Outlays	Returns	Outlays	Returns
	£	£	£	£
Time 0	2,000	800		
Year 1		800		
Year 2		800		
Year 3		800		
Year 4		800	1,600	
Year 5				1,200
Year 6				1,200
Year 7				1,200
Year 8				1,200

In this case the profitability of the first project is about 21 per cent and that of the second more than 50 per cent.

If the second outlay is obligatory, then the situation is different again. We have, in effect, one project with the following cash flows—

	Outlays	Returns
	£	£
Time 0	2,000	
Year 1		800
Year 2		800
Year 3		800
Year 4	800	–
Year 5		1,200
Year 6		1,200
Year 7		1,200
Year 8		1,200

This is a problem that cannot be handled in a straightforward way. Where a project involves one or more years during which, after some cash receipts have been obtained, there is an excess of payments over receipts, the yield method will give a false answer: in some cases there will be more than one rate of return at which the present values of the outgoing and returns are equivalent.

A suggested solution is to use a "crutch" rate. Since the situation is an unusual one, the method is not illustrated here, but briefly, the technique is to take the year in which there is an excess of payments over receipts as Time 0.

The previous payments and receipts are evaluated at, say, 10 per cent and then subsequent receipts are evaluated to find the rate at which they are equivalent to the previous payments and receipts.

A second "crutch" rate trial is then made, using say 5 per cent. If the first trial shows 15 per cent and the second 17 per cent, the true yield lies between these.

TAX CONSIDERATIONS

As was stated on page 43, tax is a cash outgoing which must be deducted in calculating the returns on a project.

CORPORATION TAX

The present basis of company taxation is that companies are liable to a corporation tax of 40 per cent of their profits as calculated according to the income tax rules.

INCOME TAX

Dividends paid to shareholders and, in some circumstances, company earnings after deduction of corporation tax are subject to income tax at the prevailing rate (8s. 3d. in the £1 in 1967/68).

CAPITAL ALLOWANCES AND INVESTMENT GRANTS

From time to time, capital allowances are given and these are charged against profits so that the impact of corporation and income tax is reduced. In 1966, investment grants were introduced and are payable instead of capital allowances.

Investment Grants

Investment grants are payable by the Board of Trade on assets used in manufacturing and extractive industries in Great Britain. Manufacturing covers all stages of processing materials up to the finished article but would not generally cover service activities or construction. Extraction covers quarrying, mining and the extraction of natural mineral deposits carried on in the course of trade. Imports will rank equally with home-produced goods.

The general rate of investment grant in 1966 was 20 per cent of the amount invested (increased to 25 per cent for 1967 and 1968 in November, 1966).

In development areas the grant was increased to 40 per cent of the capital investment (increased to 45 per cent for 1967 and 1968 in November, 1966).

Grants were payable in respect of (*a*) plant and machinery used for manufacturing and extractive purposes and (*b*) certain types of mobile equipment commonly used in manufacturing. For instance, fork-lift trucks will be eligible for grants where they are used in manufacturing or extraction.

No grants will be paid in respect of building structures and works except where these are built in development districts. In this case the normal rate is 25 per cent provided it could be shown that an adequate amount of employment in the district will be provided. The Board of Trade may also increase this grant up to 25 per cent if it is convinced that the problems involved in building will justify additional assistance.

The above provisions also apply to plant and machinery used for scientific research provided it is in relation to a qualifying process. New buildings for scientific research qualify whether in relation to a qualifying process or not.

It can be seen that vehicles also do not, in general, qualify. Two types of assets are dealt with as special cases. These are ships and computers, both of which attract an investment grant of 20 per cent provided they are new.

Investment grants are not given for office machinery and furniture, canteen equipment, loose tools and small short-lived items and there is also a minimum value of £25 below which grants will not be paid.

Since a great deal of investment is excluded from receiving investment grants, it should be stressed that such investment attracts capital allowances for tax purposes, so that the full cost of capital expenditure can ultimately be charged as costs.

Capital Allowances

These allowances are as follows—

Initial Allowance. This is a special allowance of 30 per cent of the cost of an asset as given at the time of acquisition. It is paid only if the asset is not eligible for Investment grant.

Annual Allowances. Annual allowances are given on a stipulated percentage of the written-down value, and these rates are based on the expected normal working life of the particular assets.

The 1963 Finance Act stipulates the rates allowed on investments; they are as follows—

15 per cent on investment with 18 years' life or more (minimum).

20 per cent on investment with 14–18 years' life.

25 per cent on investment with less than 14 years' life (maximum).

It is possible for a firm to claim the capital allowances using a straight-line method of depreciation (the rates are then $6\frac{1}{4}$ per cent, $8\frac{1}{2}$ per cent and $11\frac{1}{4}$ per cent), but this is an unwise policy to adopt since the normal rates give heavier allowances in the earlier years and, as we have seen, savings now are worth more than savings in the future.

There is no requirement for British companies to bring the depreciation they charge in their accounts into line with the capital allowances they receive from the Inland Revenue. A company may, in fact, claim the full allowances but choose to charge lower (or higher) rates of depreciation in their accounts.

Balancing Allowances and Charges. If an asset is disposed of for a higher price than the book value remaining after the capital allowances are deducted from the original cost, then there will be a balancing charge in respect of the difference. If the price is lower, then there will be a balancing allowance.

The effect is that the full difference between the original cost and the eventual disposal price is given in capital allowances.

Hire Purchase. Where equipment is bought under a hire-purchase agreement the normal rate of investment grant, including the development district grant, will be paid to the purchaser if the assets would otherwise qualify. Otherwise, capital allowances may be claimed.

Leased Assets. Leased assets will, similarly, attract the investment grants and capital allowances provided they would otherwise be eligible for them. They must be leased new and must be used in manufacturing or extraction for a minimum period of three years to attract investment grants.

The investment grant will be paid to the lessor who will be required to notify the Board of Trade if the equipment ceases to be used in manufacturing or extraction, or if its place is moved when it is originally in a development district. In such circumstances the lessor will be liable to repay any grant in respect of the equipment. He will also be allowed the capital allowances.

Certain institutions, such as Local Authorities and the nationalized undertakings are not eligible for investment grants. The reason for this is that the Government controls their capital expenditure in any case. This does mean, however, that the firms offering lease facilities will not be able to allow for the payment of investment grant in respect of assets leased by such bodies.

The qualifying period also applies to plant and machinery which is bought outright. That is, it must be used for at least three years in manufacturing or extraction. If it is not, then the grants allowed will be repayable.

Industrial Buildings. These attract capital allowances at a lower rate than plant and machinery. Commercial offices, premises, shops and hotels or houses do not attract allowances,

Patents. The cost is allowable, but spread over the life of the patent which may be up to seventeen years.

Mines, Oil Wells, etc. Capital allowances are made in respect of exploration costs.

Scientific Research. All the cost is allowable in the year in which the expenditure occurs.

THE TIMING OF TAXATION

It is not possible to go fully into the problems of the actual timing of allowances, but, in practice, the payment of tax on profits lags behind the making of those profits.

The Inland Revenue year runs from 6th April to 5th April of the following calendar year.

Corporation tax in the year 1967–8 will be assessed on the profits made in the previous year 1966–7. If, as is likely, a company has a different year for accounting purposes, ending say, 31st December, then the profit for the tax year will be calculated by apportioning the accounting profits. For 1966–7, the revenue will take three-quarters of the company's profits in 1965 plus one quarter of the profits in 1966.

Tax assessed in 1966–7 is payable on 1st January, 1967 although it may be paid in two instalments, the second being on 1st July, 1967.

On average, it may be said that there will be a delay of eighteen months before investment grants are received and before corporation tax is actually paid. Income tax deducted from dividends is payable, however, within one month.

Since this is the case, the value of cash grants should be discounted in the usual way.

Where cash returns from a project are uniform, the effect of tax will be to make them uneven: the initial flows being affected by the heavier initial tax allowances. This can make the process of evaluation of projects more laborious.

To cope with this problem, special tables are available which incorporate the tax factors. These are used as follows—

1. *Present Value of Cash Grant and Capital Allowances*. If the investment is £200,000 and attracts a 20 per cent cash grant and 25 per cent annual allowance on the reducing balance, the factor at a 10 per cent discount rate is 0·3913.

The present value of the allowances is £200,000 × 0·3913 = £78,260.

The cost of the asset after tax is therefore—

£200,000 − £78,260 = £221,740.

2. *Present Value of Gross Cash Flow*. If the gross cash flow is £40,000 over ten years, the gross present value can be calculated from Table B. At 10 per cent it is—

£40,000 × 6·145 = £245,800.

The effective tax factor is 0·6533 and the present value of the net cash flows will be £245,800 × 0·6533 = £162,500.

These tables may be found in *Capital Budgeting and Company Finance*, Merrett and Sykes, Longmans, 1966, and also in *Investment Appraisal*, L. Kingshott, Ford Motor Company, 1967.

EFFECT OF CASH GRANTS ON LEASING RATES

The leasing rates should vary according to—

1. Whether the equipment qualifies for investment grants or not.

2. Whether the expenditure is in a development district or not.

Example

By way of example let us use the earlier example (page 78) of a proposed leasing arrangement. The firm was faced with the opportunity to invest £800 in an asset which had a life of five years and which would bring an annual cash return of £300 after all running costs had been met.

1. *Is the project profitable?* As the earnings are uniform it is possible to find the rate of return from Table B (cumulative discount tables) by dividing the annual earnings into the investment—

$$£\frac{800}{300} = 2{\cdot}6 \text{ Factor}$$

We know the life, and we search across Table B at the five-year row for the discount rate at which 2·6 appears. It is approximately 27 per cent. This is the internal rate of return of the project.

Alternatively, if the firm knows the profitability it requires, let us say 20 per cent, then we can use the factor to calculate how long we must be able to use the asset. This is done by going down the 20 per cent column until the factor 2·6 is found. The nearest period is 4 years. The asset must be kept for a very small time beyond that period.

2. *If the project is profitable as it stands, what is the effect of an investment grant?* The plant is qualifying at the rate of 20 per cent, so that the initial capital outlay is reduced to £640. The factor is—

$$£\frac{640}{300} = 2{\cdot}13$$

and Table B shows this to have increased the profitability to more than 35 per cent. If the company profit requirement is 20 per cent then the equipment would only require to have a life of a little over three years.

If the plant is in a development area and qualifies for a cash grant of 40 per cent, then the project will involve a net initial outlay of £480.

The factor is—

$$£\frac{480}{300} = 1{\cdot}6$$

and with a five-year life the profitability shoots to over 50 per cent. With a company profit requirement of 20 per cent, the life would have to be only a little more than two years.

Having answered the question: "Is the project profitable?" we can now turn to the question of how best to finance it.

In this example the cash grants are treated as receivable at the time of the expenditure since it is the ultimate intention that this should be the case. At the time of going to press there is a twelve-month delay which reduces the value of grants.

The firm has a number of alternatives—

1. Lease—over five years, sixty monthly rentals of £2 5s. per month per £100 of cost.

2. Hire purchase—25 per cent deposit, 8½ per cent interest charge on balances, repayments in equal instalments over two years.

3. Bank borrowing—at 7½ per cent.

Lease Financing

The fact that the lease is payable in monthly instalments will have some effect on the cost of the capital, but this may be ignored unless a border-line case should be considered. Tables showing the annual value of £1 received in monthly instalments are available.

The leasing proposition is as follows—

Time 0	Borrow £800		
			£
Year 1		Lease payments (£2. 5s. × 12 × 8)	216
Year 2			216
Year 3			216
Year 4			216
Year 5			216

In this case the factor is—

$$£\frac{800}{216} = 3{\cdot}7$$

and Table B shows that the cost of borrowing £800 on these terms is about 11 per cent.

Hire Purchase

The calculation of the hire purchase instalments is—

	£
Cost of asset	800
25% Deposit paid	200
Amount borrowed	600
Interest for two years at $8\frac{1}{2}$%	102
Amount repayable	£702
Annual instalments	£351

The proposition, therefore, is—

		£
Time 0	Borrow £600	
Year 1	H.P. repayments	351
Year 2		351

Notice that the repayments would exceed the net cash return of £300 in the first two years.

The factor is—

$$£\frac{600}{351} = 1 \cdot 7$$

over two years. Reference to Table B shows that the real cost of this borrowing is again about 11 per cent. This is the same as the cost of leasing. Apart from the difficulty of meeting payments in the first two years, it has the advantage of giving the firm ownership of the assets. The ultimate disposal value of the asset reduces the cost of borrowing in this case.

Bank Borrowing

Since the bank interest will be payable only on the outstanding balance of the loan, the actual rate of interest will also be the rate quoted, $7\frac{1}{2}$ per cent.

EFFECT OF INVESTMENT GRANTS

The effect of the cash grants on these methods is shown below. The cost of leased capital would go up to 20 per cent and 35 per cent if the benefit of grants were not passed on to the users of equipment. The cost of hire purchase, however, is unchanged since, as owners, the users would be able to claim the grants.

EFFECTS OF CASH GRANTS

	LEASE				H.P.			
Level of grant	20%		40%		20%		40%	
	£	£	£	£	£	£	£	£
Time 0								
Borrow	640		480		480		360	
Year 1		Pay 216		Pay 216		Pay 281		Pay 210
		Pay 216		Pay 216		Pay 281		Pay 210
Year 3		Pay 216		Pay 216		—		—
Year 4		Pay 216		Pay 216		—		—
Year 5		Pay 216		Pay 216		—		—
Cost of capital					Cost of capital			
		20%		35%		11%		11%
	$\frac{£640}{£216} = 2{\cdot}9$		$\frac{£480}{£216} = 2{\cdot}2$		$\frac{£480}{£281} = 1{\cdot}7$		$\frac{£360}{£281} = 1{\cdot}7$	

ADJUSTMENT OF LEASE RATES

With this in mind, it is possible to look at the example in another way. If the lessors wish to maintain their return on capital, but not to increase it, what adjustments should they make to their lease rates?

The calculation is fairly simple if the cash flows are uniform. The rate at which £800 was borrowed by leasing was 11 per cent and the factor was 3·7.

If cash grant of 20 per cent is received, then the amount borrowed is reduced to £640.

Now we know that—

$$\frac{\text{Capital}}{\text{Annual cash flow}} = \text{Factor}$$

or—

$\frac{£800}{£261} = 3{\cdot}7$ which gives a satisfactory return of 11 per cent.

The problem we now have is—

$$\frac{\text{Capital}}{\text{Annual cash flows}} = \frac{£640}{\chi} = 3{\cdot}7$$

This is because, if the lessors merely wish to maintain their profitability over the five years, they can do so if the factor remains the same.

The problem can be solved by dividing the capital sum by the factor—

$$£\frac{640}{3 \cdot 7} = £173 \text{ per annum}$$

The customer should expect the lease payment to be reduced from £261 to £173 per annum if he is to get the full benefit of the 20 per cent cash grant.

What if the cash grant is 40 per cent? In this case, the calculation is—

$$£\frac{480}{3 \cdot 7} = £130 \text{ per annum}$$

In other words, the 40 per cent cash grant on a contract running over five years would half the lease payment.

THE IRRELEVANCE OF BOOK VALUES

In Chapter I the effect of depreciation on accounting profit was shown, with an example of plant costing £10,000, written off over ten years and having a residual value of £1,000. An annual charge of £900 was made against profits and the book value of the plant at any time, before it was disposed of, would be—

Original cost less depreciation = book value. At the end of, Year 3, for example, the book value would be—

	£
Original cost	10,000
less three years' depreciation at £900 per annum .	2,700
Book value	£7,300

In the earlier example, the asset was sold at the end of the third year for £1,000. As was pointed out, it is the original estimates of the life of the asset which were wrong.

Given that revenues were £3,000 per year, the results were—

1. The original payment of £10,000 in capital investment.

2. The receipt of £3,000 per year in savings or revenues for three years total £900.

3. The receipt of £1,000 cash on sale of the equipment at the end of its life.

The investment was not successful but, of course, hindsight is no substitute for foresight and no business man would allow the fact that he has made a mistake in the past to inhibit him from making predictions about the future and from looking at new equipment to replace the old.

The book value is irrelevant to decisions about the future: all that is relevant at the end of Year 3 is the £1,000 cash proceeds which the plant will bring if it is sold. These proceeds must include the cash value of an allowances for "tax losses."

The original predictions were that the asset would have a life of ten years, and the profitability then appeared satisfactory. At a stipulated rate of return of 20 per cent, the project would have shown a present-value profit of £2,995, as can be seen below—

		Investment	Annual Savings	Present Value at 20%
		£	£	£
Time 0	Capital investment	10,000		
Year 1			3,000	
Year 2			3,000	
Year 3			3,000	
Year 4			3,000	
Year 5			3,000	
Year 6			3,000	
Year 7			3,000	
Year 8			3,000	
Year 9			3,000	
Year 10			3,000	
			30,000	12,576
	Scrap value of equipment		1,000	419
	Present value of returns at 20%			12,995

INCREASED SAVINGS

At the end of Year 3 the firm is offered a new piece of equipment that promises to increase the savings to £5,000 per year and this requires a capital investment of £6,000. The new equipment will have a life of seven years and will be disposed of at the end of that time for £2,000. If the old equipment is disposed of at the end of three years it will only fetch £1,000. This shows that our original investment will not have proved worth while if we make this decision to buy new equipment.

We might, in fact, be tempted to say that since the new equipment will cost £6,000 and it could mean an accounting loss of £6,300, then it could not be worth while.

Mistaken Approach

This approach is mistaken, because the problem of the new machine is not related to the depreciation which merely tells us the way we have looked at our investment in the old machine: it is only related to the possible cash flows or increases in cash flows which it will generate during its life if we buy it.

Correct Approach

The correct appraisal (assuming that taxation has been taken into account) is—

New equipment costing—£6,000. Increase in annual savings—£2,000. Anticipated scrap value at end of life—£2,000. Anticipated life—7 years.

		Investment	Increase in Annual Savings	Present Value at 20%
		£	£	£
Year 3	Capital investment	6,000		
	less disposal proceeds (old equipment)	1,000		
		£5,000		
Year 4			2,000	
Year 5			2,000	
Year 6			2,000	
Year 7			2,000	
Year 8			2,000	
Year 9			2,000	
Year 10			2,000	
	New equipment sold for		2,000	
			£16,000	
	Present value of returns at 20%			£5,767

At a 20 per cent required earnings rate the net investment of £5,000 will show a present-value profit of £767 and the old machine should be replaced.

EFFECT OF TAXATION

Suppose, in the example, that tax had not been taken into account, what would be the change in the appraisal which would result from the tax allowances?

Let us suppose that the new machine attracts an investment grant of 25 per cent and an annual allowance of 25 per cent on the diminishing value, and that it is bought by a company paying corporation tax at 40 per cent.

The book value of the old equipment for tax purposes is also relevant. Let us assume it is £800. Since the machine is sold for £1,000, there will be a balancing charge of £200.

The calculation of the capital allowances is shown below—A charge is shown in brackets.

		£	£
Start of project (Year 3) Balancing charge (old machine)			(200)
New machine	Cost	6,000	
Investment grant (new machine)		1,500	1,500
Year 4 Capital allowance 25% of Residual value		4,500	1,125
		1,125	
Year 5 Capital allowance 25% of Residual value		3,375	844
		844	
Year 6 Capital allowance 25% of Residual value		2,531	633
		633	
Year 7 Capital allowance 25% of Residual value		1,898	474
		474	
Year 8 Capital allowance 25% of Residual value		1,424	355
		355	
Year 9 Capital allowance 25% of Residual value		1,069	267
		267	
Year 10 Capital allowance 25% of Residual value		802	200
		200	
Residual value		602	

Sold for	£2,000
Residual value	602
Balancing charge	(1,398)

If we assume that the benefit of both investment grants and capital allowances is received after one year's delay, the cash flows of the project can be calculated year by year.

	Before-tax Cash (Outlays) and Returns	Capital Allowances and (Charges)	Taxable Returns and (Allowances)	Tax at 40%	After-tax (Outlays) and Returns
	£	£			£
Year 3	(5,000)	–			5,000
Year 4	2,000	1,300	700	280	1,720
Year 5	2,000	1,125	875	350	1,650
Year 6	2,000	844	1,156	462	1,538
Year 7	2,000	633	1,367	547	1,453
Year 8	2,000	474	1,526	610	1,390
Year 9	2,000	355	1,645	658	1,342
Year 10	2,000	267	1,733	693	1,307
Year 11	—	(1,198)	(1,198)	(478)	(479)

	After-tax (Outlays) and Returns	20% Factor	Net Present Value	
	£		£	
Year 4	1,720	0·833	1,430	
Year 5	1,650	·694	1,145	
Year 6	1,538	·579	890	
Year 7	1,453	·482	700	
Year 8	1,390	·402	560	
Year 9	1,342	·335	450	
Year 10	1,307	·279	365	
				5,540
Year 11	(479)	·233	(111)	111
				£5,429

The project is still worth while as it shows a net present-value profit at 20 per cent but this is reduced to £429, as compared to £5,767 in the appraisal before tax.

6 Procedures for Capital Expenditure Authorization and Control

It is essential to effective financial management that clear and efficient procedures for the evaluation of capital expenditure be set up.

Authorization of capital expenditure should be made at a high level in a business. However, all levels of management may be given authority to make capital expenditures up to a specified amount. Such managers should be provided with appraisal forms into which they can enter their calculations of capital costs and savings so that a simple calculation of yield or net present value can be made. The rate of return required should be notified to managers and the calculation of net present-value profit will indicate which projects are acceptable.

As the amount of capital expenditure required for a project increases, so the project will be appraised by a higher level of management until the largest are taken to the Board.

AUTHORIZATION LEVELS

One scheme of capital authorization used in a large British company uses the following levels of authorization—

1. *Projects not exceeding £200.* Departmental manager (36 posts are listed).

2. *Projects not exceeding £500.* Area manager (6 posts are listed).

3. *Projects not exceeding £1,000.* General managers of regions (7 posts are listed).

4. *Projects not exceeding £2,000.* Financial director (including all service departments except Personnel), commercial director, chief engineer, personnel director, production director.

5. *Projects not exceeding £20,000.* Capital Expenditure Authorization Committee.

6. *Projects exceeding £20,000.* Board of Directors. Where a proposal to spend this amount of money is urgent, the Chairman may act for the Board between meetings.

THE CAPITAL EXPENDITURE AUTHORIZATION COMMITTEE
In the scheme quoted, this committee is composed of the four Directors and the Chief Engineer plus the Chief Economics Adviser who also acts as Secretary. In other companies, the Chief Accountant may be the technical adviser and secretary. The committee sits weekly and members may be represented by their deputies. If requested by a member of the committee, other managers or specialists may be called in to give advice on specific projects.

CONTROL OF LEASE, HIRE-PURCHASE AND RENTAL AGREEMENTS

These should be subject to normal capital authorization procedures according to the capital cost if the asset were purchased. It may also be desirable to specify that equipment taken on free trial or loan should be accepted only if authorized at the appropriate capital expenditure level.

PROPOSALS FOR CAPITAL EXPENDITURE

Part of every manager's duties is to search for new projects which will be profitable to his company and he should maintain a file in which he records ideas for projects, however vague.

A periodical review of these projects should be made and this involves forecasting the net cash outlays and returns which the project would involve. The manager should be able to make a rough assessment of the rate of return and where this seems promising, a formal proposal should be submitted to the appropriate level of authorization.

The finance department should maintain long- and short-term capital expenditure budgets but the long-term budget need not be a very formal document. As projects are brought forward into the short-term budgets, so will they be given more formal appraisal if this is called for.

COST OF APPRAISAL

The formality of an appraisal, and the amount of effort which is put into predicting the cash flows, analysing the risks, and choosing between the alternatives must be related to the capital cost of the project (or the group of projects if it is a repetitive expenditure). An expenditure of £10,000 on planning and appraisal can easily be justified on a £1,000,000 project: it is inconceivable on a £15,000 project. A word of warning, however! If the £15,000 project is repeated a hundred times, the type of project will have involved expenditure of £1,500,000, so it may, in that case, be worth spending £10,000 on appraisal of the first project.

CAPITAL EXPENDITURE AUTHORIZATION MANUAL

The first essential in any system of capital authorization and control is a manual incorporating the procedures and information adopted.

Such a manual may deal with the following topics—

1. The general purposes of capital expenditure authorization and control procedures.
2. The methods of appraisal to be adopted by the firm. The definition of capital expenditure and the specification of current expenditures which fall within the control. Definition of types of project.
3. The procedures for submitting forecasts of capital expenditure.
4. A list of authorization levels.
5. A statement of the procedure to be followed in making submissions and in authorizing projects.
6. Procedures to be followed in subsequent control of the expenditures.
7. A *pro forma* request for authorization, with instructions for its completion.

Each of these is considered in turn.

GENERAL PURPOSES

The objectives of capital evaluation is to maintain an adequate rate of return on the capital employed by the firm. This requires the control of capital and some revenue expenditure, including investments outside the firm and the purchase of shares or control of another business. Disposal of surplus assets, or assets which are being uneconomically used also comes under the procedure. Generally, the procedure may also be concerned with rationing capital between projects and ensuring that sufficient funds are available for the projects adopted.

A final objective is to control spending within the limits authorized and to check whether the anticipated profitability is achieved or not.

METHODS OF APPRAISAL

The assets covered by the procedure include all kinds of fixed and current assets.

In addition to level of authorization, projects must be classified according to type of spending. If the categories suggested in Chapter III are followed, the list might be—

Class A	New products
Class B	New designs
Class C	Expansion to meet demand
Class D	Cost saving
Class E	Replacement of plant
Class F	Welfare—obligatory
Class G	Welfare—optional

Assets made by the firm's own staff must be included although the level of authorization may be related to the direct costs of labour and materials (that is, ignoring overheads). Associated and ancillary equipment should be included.

Both pay-back and the D.C.F. appraisal methods may be used.

PROCEDURES FOR SUBMITTING FORECASTS

These should lay down the dates by which forecasts for the following financial year should be submitted and should indicate the dates by which authorization or rejection should have been notified.

The forecast should be made on a form for each project drawn up in a standard way so that proper forecasts of capital required, cash returns and the incidence of tax can be clearly shown. Full technical data should be submitted by engineers and marketing men involved in the project so that the final decision is made on all the data. Uniformity of submission and analysis is essential if consistent results are to be obtained. A suitable form is shown on page 109.

AUTHORIZATION LEVELS

A suitable list has already been illustrated on page 107. Naturally, this will vary according to the size and management structure of the individual firm.

On authorization, a project should be given an identifying code which will ensure that all the costs and revenues associated with it are properly recorded. A time limit for starting and completing a project should be laid down and any failure to live up to these dates should result in a "re-authorization" procedure.

The point at which supplementary authorizations should be requested may also be indicated. If the spending exceeds estimates by 5 per cent, then a supplementary authorization should be required.

PROCEDURE FOR SUBMISSIONS

Only submissions on the appropriate form should be accepted. The number of copies required and the normal day of submission must be stipulated, e.g. projects to be discussed at Committee on Friday should be in the hands of the secretary of the Committee by Wednesday.

On authorization, the person responsible for spending the funds should receive a signed copy of the submission and he is then responsible for getting the project under way.

Certain propositions may require approval in principle, e.g. to buy a property in a certain location for agreed purposes and, in this case, the limits of money to be spent must be clearly stipulated.

CONTROL

The financial director should be responsible for follow-up of projects to check that the funds were properly spent and to compare the actual with the predicted outcome.

The capital expenditure authorization committee may want to see a monthly list of projects approved and the results to date. Some firms analyse the results of projects according to the section from which they originate and this enables the "good guessers" to be identified. The optimists may need to be curbed a little: the pessimists to be encouraged.

Such checks are a useful technique for ensuring that careful and responsible forecasts of returns are made. They may also lead to improved forecasts by the elimination of errors. Also, managers responsible for operating plant and equipment may take action to improve the profitability if they see that a project is not achieving its objectives.

Some procedures incorporate a "control" section on the authorization *pro forma.*

NEED FOR TRAINING

No evaluation procedure will work unless those responsible for operating to it understand the general approach which is being used. Whilst the detailed appraisal of the yield or present value of a large project must be put in the hands of the economists or finance section of the firm, it is essential for all managers to be given some training in evaluation methods, along the lines indicated in this book.

Good evaluation will be impossible if the way of thinking about projects is not shared. Failure to give this training can only result in misunderstandings and bad feelings. If uncorrected, this may lead to a situation where the supply of good projects from below "dries up."

XYZ Ltd.

Request for capital expenditure/disposal

	Serial Number...............
Submitted by...........................	Factory ....
Counter-signed by..................	Area................................
	Region............................

1. CAPITAL REQUIRED £100,000

Type of project: Class A

Installation of plant for production of hollowware. Range of stainless steel products as stipulated in attached list.

Latest date of starting 31/12/67 — Latest date of completion of installation 31/3/68

2. CAPITAL REQUIRED	1967	1968	1969
Equipment	....	60,000	....
Installation expenses	....	5,000	....
Total to be authorized		65,000	
Working capital	....	35,000	....
Grand total		100,000	
ASSETS REPLACED			
Equipment	....	Nil	....
Working capital	....	Nil	....

3. FORECAST RETURNS (at level requesting authorization)

		Head Office Adjustments		
	Year	Net returns at this level			Net returns
		£	£	£	£
1	1968				
2	1969				
3	1970				
4					
5					
6					
7					
8					
9					
10					

Pay out............................years Net Present value at........% £........
Yield ....per cent.

4. AUTHORIZATION

Level at which authorized....................*Capital Authorization Committee*
Submitted at that level by....................*Production Director* on *1st Nov.*, 1967
Authorization (signed) ....*Secretary to Capital Authorization*
....*Committee* on *1st Nov.*, 1967
Rejected ....on.......................Reasons ....
Deferred ....on....................... ....
....
....

DESIGN OF A SYSTEM

Design of a system of capital authorization must always take into account the peculiarities of the company within which it is to operate but certain principles should be observed in all cases.

1. If possible, one simple request for authorization should be designed for the use of managers requesting capital.

2. The economic data required should be cash outlays and cash returns. Adjustment of these for taxation should be done by the finance department.

3. Requests for authorization should come from the managers of departments who will be responsible for implementing the proposals, if accepted.

4. A clear statement of the levels at which authorization will take place and the persons responsible is necessary. All authorizations must be signed by the responsible manager, director or secretary of Committee.

5. Regular follow-up is necessary to exercise control. This will affect current operating efficiency and improve future forecasting.

6. Training in the thinking behind the system is necessary at all levels. The finance department should be ready to assist in the preparation of proposals for spending so as to minimize loss of time and effort on unsuitable and uneconomic projects.

7. The firm must stress the positive aspect of capital budgeting. A strong and vital company should have a steady supply of new projects undergoing appraisal. It must be recognized at all levels that the profitable projects are the most desirable. Spending on desirable but unprofitable projects is possible only if this remains a minor part of the company's activity. It is possible only if other, profitable, projects are being undertaken.

TABLE A
PRESENT VALUE FACTORS

To determine the present value of a single payment received "n" years from the present (or vice versa)

Years	1%	2%	3%	4%	5%	6%	7%	8%	9%	10%
1	·9901	·9804	·9709	·9615	·9524	·9434	·9346	·9259	·9174	·9091
2	·9803	·9612	·9426	·9426	·9070	·8900	·8734	·8573	·8417	·8264
3	·9706	·9423	·9151	·8890	·8638	·8396	·8163	·7938	·7722	·7513
4	·9610	·9238	·8885	·8548	·8227	·7921	·7629	·7350	·7084	·6830
5	·9515	·9057	·8626	·8219	·7835	·7473	·7130	·6806	·6499	·6209
6	·9420	·8880	·8375	·7903	·7462	·7050	·6663	·6302	·5963	·5645
7	·9327	·8706	·8131	·7599	·7107	·6651	·6227	·5835	·5470	·5132
8	·9235	·8535	·7894	·7307	·6768	·6274	·5820	·5403	·5019	·4665
9	·9143	·8368	·7664	·7026	·6446	·5919	·5439	·5002	·4604	·4241
10	·9053	·8203	·7441	·6756	·6139	·5584	·5083	·4632	·4224	·3855
11	·8963	·8043	·7224	·6496	·5847	·5268	·4751	·4289	·3875	·3505
12	·8874	·7885	·7014	·6246	·5568	·4970	·4440	·3971	·3555	·3186
13	·8787	·7730	·6810	·6006	·5303	·4688	·4150	·3677	·3262	·2897
14	·8700	·7579	·6611	·5775	·5051	·4423	·3878	·3405	·2992	·2633
15	·8613	·7430	·6419	·5553	·4810	·4173	·3624	·3152	·2745	·2394
16	·8528	·7284	·6232	·5339	·4581	·3936	·3387	·2919	·2519	·2176
17	·8444	·7142	·6050	·5134	·4363	·3714	·3166	·2703	·2311	·1978
18	·8360	·7002	·5874	·4936	·4155	·3503	·2959	·2502	·2120	·1799
19	·8277	·6864	·5703	·4746	·3957	·3305	·2765	·2317	·1945	·1635
20	·8195	·6730	·5537	·4564	·3769	·3118	·2584	·2145	·1784	·1486
21	·8114	·6598	·5375	·4388	·3589	·2942	·2415	·1987	·1637	·1351
22	·8034	·6468	·5219	·4220	·3418	·2775	·2257	·1839	·1502	·1228
23	·7954	·6342	·5067	·4057	·3256	·2618	·2109	·1703	·1378	·1117
24	·7876	·6217	·4919	·3901	·3101	·2470	·1971	·1577	·1264	·1015
25	·7798	·6095	·4776	·3751	·2953	·2330	·1842	·1460	·1160	·0923
26	·7720	·5976	·4637	·3607	·2812	·2198	·1722	·1352	·1064	·0839
27	·7644	·5859	·4502	·3468	·2678	·2074	·1609	·1252	·0976	·0763
28	·7568	·5744	·4371	·3335	·2551	·1956	·1504	·1159	·0895	·0693
29	·7493	·5631	·4243	·3207	·2429	·1846	·1406	·1073	·0822	·0630
30	·7419	·5521	·4120	·3083	·2314	·1741	·1314	·0994	·0754	·0573
31	·7346	·5412	·4000	·2965	·2204	·1643	·1228	·0920	·0691	·0521
32	·7273	·5306	·3883	·2851	·2099	·1550	·1147	·0852	·0634	·0474
33	·7201	·5202	·3770	·2741	·1999	·1462	·1072	·0789	·0582	·0431
34	·7130	·5100	·3660	·2636	·1904	·1379	·1002	·0730	·0534	·0391
35	·7059	·5000	·3554	·2534	·1813	·1301	·0937	·0676	·0490	·0356
36	·6989	·4902	·3450	·2437	·1727	·1227	·0875	·0626	·0449	·0323
37	·6920	·4806	·3350	·2343	·1644	·1158	·0818	·0580	·0412	·0294
38	·6852	·4712	·3252	·2253	·1566	·1092	·0765	·0537	·0378	·0267
39	·6784	·4619	·3158	·2166	·1491	·1031	·0715	·0497	·0347	·0243
40	·6717	·4529	·3066	·2083	·1420	·0972	·0668	·0460	·0318	·0221
41	·6650	·4440	·2976	·2003	·1353	·0917	·0624	·0426	·0292	·0210
42	·6584	·4353	·2890	·1926	·1288	·0865	·0583	·0395	·0268	·0183
43	·6519	·4268	·2805	·1852	·1227	·0816	·0545	·0365	·0246	·0166
44	·6454	·4184	·2724	·1780	·1169	·0770	·0509	·0338	·0226	·0151
45	·6391	·4102	·2644	·1712	·1113	·0727	·0476	·0313	·0207	·0137
46	·6327	·4022	·2567	·1646	·1060	·0685	·0445	·0290	·0190	·0125
47	·6265	·3943	·2493	·1583	·1009	·0647	·0416	·0269	·0174	·0113
48	·6203	·3865	·2420	·1522	·0961	·0610	·0389	·0249	·0160	·0103
49	·6141	·3790	·2350	·1463	·0916	·0575	·0363	·0230	·0147	·0094
50	·6080	·3715	·2281	·1407	·0872	·0543	·0339	·0213	·0134	·0085

TABLE A

To determine the present value of a single payment received "n" years from the present (or vice versa)

Years	11%	12%	13%	14%	15%	16%	17%	18%	19%	20%
1	·9009	·8923	·8850	·8772	·8696	·8621	·8547	·8475	·8403	·8330
2	·8116	·7972	·7831	·7695	·7561	·7432	·7305	·7182	·7062	·6940
3	·7312	·7118	·6931	·6750	·6575	·6407	·6244	·6086	·5934	·5707
4	·6587	·6355	·6133	·5921	·5718	·5523	·5337	·5158	·4987	·4820
5	·5935	·5674	·5428	·5194	·4972	·4761	·4561	·4371	·4190	·4020
6	·5346	·5066	·4803	·4556	·4323	·4104	·3898	·3704	·3521	·3351
7	·4817	·4523	·4251	·3996	·3759	·3538	·3332	·3139	·2959	·2791
8	·4339	·4039	·3762	·3506	·3269	·3050	·2848	·2660	·2487	·2331
9	·3909	·3606	·3329	·3075	·2843	·2630	·2434	·2255	·2090	·1938
10	·3522	·3220	·2946	·2697	·2472	·2267	·2080	·1911	·1756	·1615
11	·3173	·2875	·2607	·2366	·2149	·1954	·1778	·1619	·1476	·1346
12	·2858	·2567	·2307	·2076	·1869	·1685	·1520	·1372	·1240	·1122
13	·2575	·2292	·2042	·1821	·1625	·1452	·1299	·1163	·1042	·0935
14	·2320	·2046	·1807	·1597	·1413	·1252	·1110	·0985	·0876	·0779
15	·2090	·1827	·1599	·1401	·1229	·1079	·0949	·0835	·0736	·0649
16	·1883	·1631	·1415	·1229	·1069	·0930	·0818	·0708	·0618	·0541
17	·1696	·1456	·1252	·1078	·0929	·0802	·0693	·0600	·0520	·0451
18	·1528	·1300	·1108	·0946	·0808	·0691	·0592	·0508	·0437	·0376
19	·1377	·1161	·0981	·0829	·0703	·0596	·0506	·0431	·0367	·0313
20	·1240	·1037	·0868	·0728	·0611	·0514	·0433	·0365	·0303	·0261
21	·1117	·0926	·0768	·0638	·0531	·0443	·0370	·0309	·0259	·0217
22	·1007	·0826	·0680	·0560	·0462	·0382	·0316	·0262	·0218	·0181
23	·0907	·0738	·0601	·0491	·0402	·0329	·0270	·0222	·0183	·0151
24	·0817	·0659	·0532	·0431	·0349	·0284	·0231	·0188	·0154	·0126
25	·0736	·0588	·0471	·0378	·0304	·0245	·0197	·0160	·0129	·0105
26	·0663	·0525	·0417	·0331	·0264	·0211	·0169	·0135	·0109	·0087
27	·0597	·0469	·0369	·0291	·0230	·0182	·0144	·0115	·0091	·0073
28	·0538	·0419	·0326	·0255	·0200	·0157	·0123	·0097	·0077	·0061
29	·0485	·0374	·0289	·0224	·0174	·0135	·0105	·0082	·0064	·0051
30	·0437	·0334	·0256	·0196	·0151	·0116	·0090	·0070	·0054	·0042
31	·0394	·0298	·0226	·0172	·0131	·0100	·0077	·0059	·0046	·0035
32	·0355	·0266	·0200	·0151	·0114	·0087	·0066	·0050	·0038	·0029
33	·0319	·0238	·0177	·0132	·0099	·0075	·0056	·0042	·0032	·0024
34	·0288	·0212	·0157	·0116	·0086	·0064	·0048	·0036	·0027	·0020
35	·0259	·0189	·0139	·0102	·0075	·0055	·0041	·0030	·0023	·0017
36	·0234	·0169	·0123	·0089	·0065	·0048	·0035	·0026	·0019	·0014
37	·0210	·0151	·0109	·0078	·0057	·0041	·0030	·0022	·0016	·0012
38	·0190	·0135	·0096	·0069	·0049	·0036	·0026	·0019	·0013	·0010
39	·0171	·0120	·0085	·0060	·0043	·0031	·0022	·0016	·0011	·0008
40	·0154	·0107	·0075	·0053	·0037	·0026	·0019	·0013	·0010	·0007
41	·0139	·0096	·0067	·0046	·0032	·0023	·0016	·0011	·0008	·0006
42	·0125	·0086	·0059	·0041	·0028	·0020	·0014	·0010	·0007	·0005
43	·0112	·0076	·0052	·0036	·0025	·0017	·0012	·0008	·0006	·0004
44	·0101	·0068	·0046	·0031	·0021	·0015	·0010	·0007	·0005	·0003
45	·0091	·0061	·0041	·0027	·0019	·0013	·0009	·0006	·0004	·0003
46	·0082	·0054	·0036	·0024	·0016	·0011	·0007	·0005	·0003	·0002
47	·0074	·0049	·0032	·0021	·0014	·0009	·0006	·0004	·0003	·0002
48	·0067	·0043	·0028	·0019	·0012	·0008	·0005	·0004	·0002	·0002
49	·0060	·0039	·0025	·0016	·0011	·0007	·0005	·0003	·0002	·0001
50	·0054	·0035	·0022	·0014	·0009	·0006	·0004	·0003	·0002	·0001

TABLE A
PRESENT VALUE FACTORS

To determine the present value of a single payment received "n" years from the present (or vice versa)

Years	21%	22%	23%	24%	25%	26%	27%	28%	29%	30%
1	·8264	·8197	·8130	·8065	·8000	·7937	·7874	·7813	·7752	·7692
2	·6830	·6719	·6610	·6504	·6400	·6299	·6200	·6104	·6009	·5917
3	·5645	·5507	·5374	·5245	·5120	·4999	·4888	·4768	·4658	·4552
4	·4665	·4514	·4369	·4230	·4096	·3968	·3844	·3725	·3611	·3501
5	·3855	·3700	·3552	·3411	·3277	·3149	·3027	·2910	·2799	·2693
6	·3186	·3033	·2888	·2751	·2621	·2499	·2383	·2274	·2170	·2072
7	·2633	·2486	·2348	·2218	·2097	·1983	·1877	·1776	·1682	·1594
8	·2176	·2038	·1909	·1789	·1678	·1574	·1478	·1388	·1304	·1226
9	·1799	·1670	·1552	·1443	·1342	·1249	·1164	·1084	·1011	·0943
10	·1486	·1369	·1262	·1164	·1074	·0992	·0916	·0847	·0784	·0725
11	·1228	·1122	·1026	·0938	·0859	·0787	·0721	·0662	·0607	·0558
12	·1015	·0920	·0834	·0757	·0687	·0625	·0568	·0517	·0471	·0429
13	·0839	·0754	·0678	·0610	·0550	·0496	·0447	·0404	·0365	·0330
14	·0693	·0618	·0551	·0492	·0440	·0393	·0352	·0316	·0283	·0254
15	·0573	·0507	·0448	·0397	·0352	·0312	·0277	·0247	·0219	·0195
16	·0474	·0415	·0364	·0320	·0281	·0248	·0218	·0193	·0170	·0150
17	·0391	·0340	·0296	·0258	·0225	·0197	·0172	·0150	·0132	·0116
18	·0323	·0279	·0241	·0208	·0180	·0156	·0135	·0118	·0102	·0089
19	·0267	·0229	·0196	·0168	·0144	·0124	·0107	·0092	·0079	·0068
20	·0221	·0187	·0159	·0135	·0115	·0098	·0084	·0072	·0061	·0053
21	·0183	·0154	·0129	·0109	·0092	·0078	·0066	·0056	·0048	·0040
22	·0151	·0126	·0105	·0088	·0074	·0062	·0052	·0044	·0037	·0031
23	·0125	·0103	·0086	·0071	·0059	·0049	·0041	·0034	·0029	·0024
24	·0103	·0085	·0070	·0057	·0047	·0039	·0032	·0027	·0022	·0018
25	·0085	·0069	·0057	·0046	·0038	·0031	·0025	·0021	·0017	·0014
26	·0070	·0057	·0046	·0037	·0030	·0025	·0020	·0016	·0013	·0011
27	·0058	·0047	·0037	·0030	·0024	·0019	·0016	·0013	·0010	·0008
28	·0048	·0038	·0030	·0024	·0019	·0015	·0012	·0010	·0008	·0006
29	·0040	·0031	·0025	·0020	·0015	·0012	·0010	·0008	·0006	·0005
30	·0033	·0026	·0020	·0016	·0012	·0010	·0008	·0006	·0005	·0004
31	·0027	·0021	·0016	·0013	·0010	·0008	·0006	·0005	·0004	·0003
32	·0022	·0017	·0013	·0010	·0008	·0006	·0005	·0004	·0003	·0002
33	·0019	·0014	·0011	·0008	·0006	·0005	·0004	·0003	·0002	·0002
34	·0015	·0012	·0009	·0007	·0005	·0004	·0003	·0002	·0002	·0001
35	·0013	·0009	·0007	·0005	·0004	·0003	·0002	·0002	·0001	·0001
36	·0010	·0008	·0006	·0004	·0003	·0002	·0002	·0001	·0001	·0001
37	·0009	·0006	·0005	·0003	·0003	·0002	·0001	·0001	·0001	·0001
38	·0007	·0005	·0004	·0003	·0002	·0002	·0001	·0001	·0001	
39	·0006	·0004	·0003	·0002	·0002	·0001	·0001	·0001	·0000	
40	·0005	·0004	·0003	·0002	·0001	·0001	·0001	·0001		
41	·0004	·0003	·0002	·0001	·0001	·0001	·0001			
42	·0003	·0002	·0002	·0001	·0001	·0001				
43	·0003	·0002	·0001	·0001	·0001					
44	·0002	·0002	·0001	·0001	·0001					
45	·0002	·0001	·0001	·0001						
46	·0002	·0001	·0001	·0001						
47	·0001	·0001	·0001							
48	·0001	·0001								
49	·0001	·0001								
50	·0001									

TABLE A
PRESENT VALUE FACTORS

To determine the present value of a single payment received "n" years from the present (or vice versa)

Years	31%	32%	33%	34%	35%	36%	37%	38%	39%	40%
1	·7634	·7576	·7519	·7463	·7407	·7353	·7299	·7246	·7194	·7143
2	·5827	·5739	·5653	·5569	·5487	·5407	·5328	·5251	·5176	·5102
3	·4448	·4348	·4251	·4156	·4064	·3975	·3889	·3805	·3724	·3644
4	·3396	·3294	·3196	·3102	·3011	·2923	·2839	·2757	·2679	·2603
5	·2592	·2495	·2403	·2315	·2230	·2149	·2072	·1998	·1927	·1859
6	·1979	·1890	·1807	·1727	·1652	·1580	·1512	·1448	·1386	·1328
7	·1510	·1432	·1358	·1289	·1224	·1162	·1104	·1049	·1997	·0949
8	·1153	·1085	·1021	·0962	·0906	·0854	·0806	·0760	·0718	·0678
9	·0880	·0822	·0768	·0718	·0671	·0628	·0588	·0551	·0516	·0484
10	·0672	·0623	·0577	·0536	·0497	·0462	·0429	·0399	·0371	·0346
11	·0513	·0472	·0434	·0400	·0368	·0340	·0313	·0289	·0267	·0247
12	·0392	·0357	·0326	·0298	·0273	·0250	·0229	·0210	·0192	·0176
13	·0299	·0271	·0245	·0223	·0202	·0184	·0167	·0152	·0138	·0126
14	·0228	·0205	·0185	·0166	·0150	·0135	·0122	·0110	·0099	·0090
15	·0174	·0155	·0139	·0124	·0111	·0099	·0089	·0080	·0072	·0064
16	·0133	·0118	·0104	·0093	·0082	·0073	·0065	·0058	·0051	·0046
17	·0101	·0089	·0078	·0069	·0061	·0054	·0047	·0042	·0037	·0033
18	·0077	·0068	·0059	·0052	·0045	·0039	·0035	·0030	·0027	·0023
19	·0059	·0051	·0044	·0038	·0033	·0029	·0025	·0022	·0019	·0017
20	·0045	·0039	·0033	·0029	·0025	·0021	·0018	·0016	·0014	·0012
21	·0034	·0029	·0025	·0021	·0018	·0016	·0013	·0012	·0010	·0009
22	·0025	·0022	·0019	·0016	·0014	·0012	·0010	·0008	·0007	·0006
23	·0020	·0017	·0014	·0012	·0010	·0008	·0007	·0006	·0005	·0004
24	·0015	·0013	·0011	·0009	·0007	·0006	·0005	·0004	·0004	·0003
25	·0012	·0010	·0008	·0007	·0006	·0005	·0004	·0003	·0003	·0002
26	·0009	·0007	·0006	·0005	·0004	·0003	·0003	·0002	·0002	·0002
27	·0007	·0006	·0005	·0004	·0003	·0002	·0002	·0002	·0001	·0001
28	·0005	·0004	·0003	·0003	·0002	·0002	·0001	·0001	·0001	·0001
29	·0004	·0003	·0003	·0002	·0002	·0001	·0001	·0001	·0001	·0001
30	·0003	·0002	·0002	·0002	·0001	·0001	·0001	·0001	·0001	
31	·0002	·0002	·0001	·0001	·0001	·0001	·0001			
32	·0002	·0001	·0001	·0001	·0001	·0001				
33	·0001	·0001	·0001	·0001	·0001					
34	·0001	·0001	·0001							
35	·0001	·0001								
36	·0001									

TABLE B
CUMULATIVE PRESENT VALUE FACTORS

Years 0 to:	1%	2%	3%	4%	5%	6%	7%	8%	9%	10%
1	·990	·980	·971	·962	·952	·943	·935	·926	·917	·909
2	1·970	1·942	1·913	1·886	1·859	1·833	1·808	1·783	1·759	1·736
3	2·941	2·884	2·829	2·775	2·723	2·673	2·624	2·577	2·531	2·487
4	3·902	3·808	3·717	3·630	3·546	3·465	3·387	3·312	3·240	3·170
5	4·853	4·713	4·580	4·452	4·329	4·212	4·100	3·993	3·890	3·791
6	5·795	5·601	5·417	5·242	5·076	4·917	4·767	4·623	4·486	4·355
7	6·728	6·472	6·230	6·002	5·786	5·582	5·389	5·206	5·033	4·868
8	7·652	7·325	7·020	6·733	6·463	6·210	5·971	5·747	5·535	5·335
9	8·566	8·162	7·786	7·435	7·108	6·802	6·515	6·247	5·995	5·759
10	9·471	8·983	8·530	8·111	7·722	7·360	7·024	6·710	6·418	6·145
11	10·378	9·787	9·253	8·760	8·306	7·887	7·499	7·139	6·805	6·495
12	11·255	10·575	9·954	9·385	8·863	8·384	7·943	7·536	7·161	6·814
13	12·134	11·348	10·635	9·986	9·394	8·853	8·358	7·904	7·487	7·103
14	13·004	12·106	11·296	10·563	9·899	9·295	8·745	8·244	7·786	7·367
15	13·865	12·849	11·938	11·118	10·380	9·712	9·108	8·559	8·061	7·606
16	14·718	13·578	12·561	11·652	10·838	10·106	9·447	8·851	8·313	7·824
17	15·562	14·292	13·166	12·166	11·274	10·477	9·763	9·122	8·544	8·022
18	16·398	14·992	13·754	12·659	11·690	10·828	10·059	9·372	8·756	8·201
19	17·226	15·678	14·324	13·134	12·085	11·158	10·336	9·604	8·950	8·365
20	18·046	16·351	14·877	13·590	12·462	11·470	10·594	9·818	9·129	8·514
21	18·857	17·011	15·415	14·029	12·821	11·764	10·836	10·017	9·292	8·649
22	19·660	17·658	15·937	14·451	13·163	12·042	11·061	10·201	9·442	8·772
23	20·456	18·292	16·444	14·857	13·489	12·303	11·272	10·371	9·580	8·883
24	21·243	18·914	16·936	15·247	13·799	12·550	11·469	10·529	9·707	8·985
25	22·023	19·523	17·413	15·622	14·094	12·783	11·654	10·675	9·823	9·077
26	22·795	20·121	17·877	15·983	14·375	13·003	11·826	10·810	9·929	9·161
27	23·560	20·707	18·327	16·330	14·643	13·211	11·987	10·935	10·027	9·237
28	24·316	21·281	18·764	16·663	14·898	13·406	12·137	11·051	10·116	9·307
29	25·066	21·844	19·188	16·984	15·141	13·591	12·278	11·158	10·198	9·370
30	25·808	22·396	19·600	17·292	15·372	13·765	12·409	11·258	10·274	9·427
31	26·542	22·938	20·000	17·588	15·593	13·929	12·532	11·350	10·343	9·479
32	27·270	23·468	20·389	17·874	15·803	14·084	12·647	11·435	10·406	9·526
33	27·990	23·989	20·766	18·148	16·003	14·230	12·754	11·514	10·464	9·569
34	28·703	24·499	21·132	18·411	16·193	14·368	12·854	11·587	10·518	9·609
35	29·409	24·999	21·487	18·665	16·374	14·498	12·948	11·655	10·567	9·644
36	30·108	25·489	21·832	18·908	16·547	14·621	13·035	11·717	10·612	9·677
37	30·780	25·969	22·167	19·143	16·711	14·737	13·117	11·775	10·653	9·706
38	31·485	26·441	22·492	19·368	16·868	14·846	13·193	11·829	10·691	9·733
39	32·163	26·903	22·808	19·584	17·017	14·949	13·265	11·879	10·726	9·757
40	32·835	27·355	23·115	19·793	17·159	15·046	13·332	11·925	10·757	9·779

TABLE B
CUMULATIVE PRESENT VALUE FACTORS

Years 0 to:	11%	12%	13%	14%	15%	16%	17%	18%	19%	20%
1	·901	·893	·885	·877	·870	·862	·855	·848	·840	·833
2	1·712	1·690	1·668	1·647	1·626	1·605	1·585	1·566	1·546	1·528
3	2·444	2·402	2·361	2·322	2·283	2·246	2·210	2·174	2·140	2·106
4	3·102	3·307	2·974	2·914	2·855	2·798	2·743	2·690	2·639	2·589
5	3·696	3·605	3·517	3·433	3·352	3·274	3·199	3·127	3·058	2·991
6	4·230	4·111	3·998	3·889	3·784	3·685	3·589	3·498	3·410	3·326
7	4·712	4·564	4·423	4·288	4·160	4·039	3·922	3·812	3·706	3·605
8	5·146	4·968	4·799	4·639	4·487	4·344	4·207	4·078	3·954	3·837
9	5·537	5·328	5·132	4·946	4·772	4·607	4·451	4·303	4·163	4·031
10	5·889	5·650	5·426	5·216	5·019	4·833	4·659	4·494	4·339	4·192
11	6·206	5·938	5·687	5·453	5·234	5·029	4·836	4·656	4·486	4·327
12	6·492	6·194	5·918	5·660	5·420	5·197	4·988	4·793	4·610	4·439
13	6·750	6·424	6·122	5·842	5·583	5·342	5·118	4·910	4·715	4·533
14	6·982	6·628	6·303	6·002	5·724	5·468	5·229	5·008	4·802	4·611
15	7·191	6·811	6·463	6·142	5·847	5·576	5·324	5·092	4·876	4·676
16	7·379	6·974	6·604	6·265	5·954	5·668	5·405	5·162	4·938	4·730
17	7·549	7·120	6·729	6·373	6·047	5·749	5·475	5·222	4·990	4·775
18	7·702	7·250	6·840	6·468	6·128	5·818	5·534	5·273	5·033	4·812
19	7·839	7·366	6·938	6·550	6·198	5·877	5·584	5·316	5·070	4·844
20	7·963	7·469	7·025	6·623	6·259	5·929	5·628	5·353	5·101	4·870
21	8·075	7·562	7·102	6·687	6·312	5·973	5·665	5·384	5·127	4·892
22	8·176	7·645	7·170	6·743	6·358	6·011	5·696	5·410	5·149	4·910
23	8·266	7·718	7·230	6·792	6·399	6·044	5·723	5·432	5·167	4·925
24	8·348	7·784	7·283	6·835	6·434	6·073	5·746	5·451	5·182	4·937
25	8·422	7·843	7·330	6·873	6·464	6·097	5·766	5·467	5·195	4·948
26	8·488	7·896	7·372	6·906	6·490	6·118	5·783	5·480	5·206	4·956
27	8·548	7·942	7·409	6·935	6·513	6·136	5·797	5·492	5·215	4·964
28	8·601	7·984	7·441	6·961	6·533	6·152	5·810	5·502	5·223	4·970
29	8·650	8·022	7·470	6·983	6·551	6·166	5·820	5·510	5·229	4·975
30	8·694	8·055	7·496	7·003	6·566	6·177	5·829	5·517	5·235	4·979
31	8·733	8·085	7·518	7·020	6·579	6·187	5·837	5·523	5·239	4·983
32	8·768	8·112	7·538	7·035	6·590	6·196	5·844	5·528	5·243	4·986
33	8·800	8·135	7·556	7·048	6·600	6·203	5·849	5·532	5·246	4·988
34	8·829	8·157	7·572	7·060	6·609	6·210	5·854	5·535	5·249	4·990
35	8·855	8·176	7·586	7·070	6·616	6·215	5·858	5·538	5·251	4·992
36	8·878	8·192	7·598	7·079	6·623	6·220	5·862	5·541	5·253	4·993
37	8·900	8·208	7·609	7·087	6·629	6·224	5·864	5·543	5·255	4·994
38	8·918	8·221	7·619	7·094	6·634	6·228	5·867	5·545	5·256	4·995
39	8·936	8·233	7·627	7·100	6·638	6·231	5·869	5·547	5·257	4·996
40	8·951	8·244	7·635	7·105	6·642	6·234	5·871	5·548	5·258	4·997

TABLE B
CUMULATIVE PRESENT VALUE FACTORS

Years 0 to:	21%	22%	23%	24%	25%	26%	27%	28%	29%	30%
1	·826	·820	·813	·806	·800	·794	·787	·781	·775	·769
2	1·509	1·492	1·474	1·457	1·440	1·424	1·407	1·392	1·376	1·361
3	2·074	2·042	2·011	1·981	1·952	1·924	1·896	1·868	1·842	1·816
4	2·540	2·494	2·448	2·404	2·362	2·320	2·280	2·241	2·203	2·166
5	2·926	2·864	2·804	2·746	2·689	2·635	2·583	2·532	2·483	2·436
6	3·244	3·167	3·092	3·021	2·951	2·885	2·821	2·759	2·670	2·643
7	3·508	3·416	3·327	3·242	3·161	3·083	3·009	2·937	2·868	2·802
8	3·725	3·619	3·518	3·421	3·329	3·241	3·156	3·076	2·998	2·925
9	3·905	3·786	3·673	3·566	3·463	3·366	3·273	3·184	3·100	3·019
10	4·054	3·923	3·799	3·682	3·570	3·465	3·364	3·269	3·178	3·092
11	4·177	4·036	3·902	3·776	3·656	3·544	3·437	3·335	3·239	3·147
12	4·278	4·128	3·985	3·852	3·725	3·606	3·493	3·387	3·286	3·190
13	4·362	4·203	4·053	3·912	3·780	3·656	3·538	3·427	3·322	3·223
14	4·431	4·265	4·108	3·962	3·824	3·695	3·573	3·459	3·351	3·249
15	4·489	4·315	4·153	4·001	3·859	3·726	3·601	3·483	3·372	3·268
16	4·536	4·357	4·190	4·033	3·887	3·751	3·623	3·503	3·390	3·283
17	4·575	4·391	4·219	4·059	3·910	3·771	3·640	3·518	3·403	3·295
18	4·608	4·419	4·243	4·080	3·928	3·786	3·654	3·530	3·413	3·304
19	4·634	4·442	4·263	4·097	3·942	3·799	3·664	3·539	3·421	3·310
20	4·656	4·460	4·279	4·110	3·954	3·808	3·673	3·546	3·427	3·316
21	4·675	4·476	4·292	4·121	3·963	3·816	3·679	3·552	3·432	3·320
22	4·690	4·488	4·302	4·130	3·970	3·822	3·684	3·556	3·435	3·323
23	4·702	4·499	4·311	4·137	3·976	3·827	3·688	3·559	3·438	3·325
24	4·712	4·507	4·318	4·143	3·981	3·831	3·692	3·562	3·440	3·327
25	4·721	4·514	4·323	4·147	3·985	3·834	3·694	3·564	3·442	3·328
26	4·728	4·520	4·328	4·151	3·988	3·837	3·696	3·566	3·443	3·329
27	4·734	4·524	4·332	4·154	3·990	3·839	3·698	3·567	3·444	3·330
28	4·739	4·528	4·335	4·156	3·992	3·840	3·699	3·568	3·445	3·331
29	4·743	4·531	4·337	4·158	3·994	3·841	3·700	3·569	3·446	3·331
30	4·746	4·534	4·339	4·160	3·995	3·842	3·701	3·570	3·446	3·332
31	4·749	4·536	4·341	4·161	3·996	3·843	3·701	3·570	3·447	3·332
32	4·751	4·538	4·342	4·162	3·997	3·844	3·702	3·571	3·447	3·332
33	4·753	4·539	4·343	4·163	3·997	3·844	3·702	3·571	3·447	3·332
34	4·754	4·540	4·344	4·164	3·998	3·845	3·703	3·571	3·448	3·333
35	4·756	4·541	4·345	4·164	3·998	3·845	3·703	3·571	3·448	3·333
36	4·756	4·542	4·345	4·165	3·998	3·845	3·703	3·571	3·448	3·333
37	4·757	4·543	4·346	4·165	3·999	3·846	3·703	3·571	3·448	3·333
38	4·758	4·543	4·346	4·165	3·999	3·846	3·703	3·571	3·448	3·333
39	4·759	4·544	4·347	4·166	3·999	3·846	3·703	3·571	4·448	3·333
40	4·759	4·544	4·347	4·166	3·999	3·846	3·703	3·572	3·448	3·333

TABLE B
CUMULATIVE PRESENT VALUE FACTORS

Years 0 to:	31%	32%	33%	34%	35%	36%	37%	38%	39%	40%
1	·763	·758	·752	·746	·741	·735	·730	·725	·719	·714
2	1·346	1·332	1·317	1·303	1·289	1·276	1·263	1·250	1·237	1·224
3	1·791	1·766	1·742	1·719	1·696	1·674	1·652	1·630	1·609	1·589
4	2·130	2·096	2·062	2·029	1·997	1·966	1·936	1·906	1·877	1·849
5	2·390	2·345	2·302	2·260	2·220	2·181	2·143	2·106	2·070	2·035
6	2·588	2·534	2·483	2·433	2·385	2·339	2·294	2·250	2·209	2·168
7	2·739	2·677	2·619	2·562	2·508	2·455	2·404	2·355	2·308	2·263
8	2·845	2·786	2·721	2·658	2·598	2·540	2·485	2·431	2·380	2·331
9	2·942	2·868	2·798	2·730	2·665	2·603	2·544	2·486	2·432	2·379
10	3·009	2·930	2·855	2·784	2·715	2·649	2·587	2·526	2·469	2·414
11	3·060	2·978	2·899	2·824	2·752	2·683	2·618	2·555	2·496	2·438
12	3·100	3·013	2·931	2·854	2·779	2·708	2·641	2·576	2·515	2·456
13	3·130	3·040	2·956	2·876	2·799	2·727	2·658	2·592	2·528	2·468
14	3·152	2·061	2·974	2·892	2·814	2·740	2·670	2·602	2·538	2·478
15	3·170	3·076	2·988	2·905	2·825	2·750	2·679	2·610	2·546	2·484
16	3·183	3·088	2·999	2·914	2·834	2·757	2·685	2·616	2·551	2·488
17	3·193	3·097	3·006	2·921	2·840	2·763	2·690	2·620	2·554	2·492
18	3·201	2·104	3·012	2·926	2·844	2·767	2·693	2·624	2·557	2·494
19	3·207	3·109	3·017	2·930	2·847	2·770	2·696	2·626	2·559	2·496
20	3·211	3·113	3·020	2·933	2·850	2·772	2·698	2·627	2·560	2·497
21	3·215	3·116	3·022	2·935	2·852	2·773	2·699	2·628	2·561	2·498
22	3·217	3·118	3·024	2·937	2·853	2·774	2·700	2·629	2·562	2·498
23	3·219	3·120	3·026	2·938	2·854	2·775	2·701	2·630	2·563	2·499
24	3·221	3·121	3·027	2·939	2·855	2·776	2·701	2·630	2·563	2·499
25	3·222	3·122	3·028	2·939	2·855	2·776	2·702	2·631	2·562	2·499
26	3·223	3·123	3·028	2·940	2·856	2·777	2·702	2·631	2·564	2·500
27	3·224	3·123	3·029	2·940	2·856	2·777	2·702			
28	3·224	3·124	3·029	2·941	2·856	2·777	2·702			
29	3·224	3·124	3·029	2·941	2·856	2·777	2·702			
30	3·225	3·124	3·030	2·941	2·857	2·777	2·702			
31	3·225	3·124	3·030	2·941	2·857	2·778	2·703			
32	3·225	3·124								
33	3·225	3·125								
34	3·225	3·125								
35	3·225	3·125								
36	3·226	3·125								
37	3·226									
38	3·226									
39	3·226									
40	3·226	3·125	3·030	2·941	2·857	2·778	2·703	2·631	2·564	2·500

TABLE C
CAPITAL RECOVERY FACTORS

To determine the series of "n" payments which will be yielded by a given sum invested now

Years	1%	2%	3%	4%	5%	6%	7%	8%	9%	10%
1	1·0100	1·0200	1·0300	1·0400	1·0500	1·0600	1·0700	1·0800	1·0900	1·1000
2	·5076	·5155	·5226	·5305	·5376	·5455	·5529	·5606	·5685	·5760
3	·3401	·3466	·3534	·3604	·3671	·3741	·3811	·3880	·3951	·4021
4	·2564	·2625	·2691	·2755	·2820	·2886	·2952	·3019	·3086	·3155
5	·2062	·2121	·2183	·2246	·2309	·2374	·2439	·2505	·2571	·2638
6	·1724	·1786	·1846	·1907	·1970	·2034	·2098	·2163	·2229	·2296
7	·1486	·1546	·1605	·1666	·1728	·1792	·1855	·1921	·1987	·2054
8	·1307	·1365	·1425	·1485	·1547	·1610	·1675	·1740	·1807	·1874
9	·1167	·1225	·1284	·1345	·1407	·1470	·1535	·1601	·1668	·1736
10	·1056	·1113	·1172	·1233	·1295	·1359	·1424	·1490	·1558	·1627
11	·0964	·1022	·1081	·1142	·1204	·1268	·1334	·1401	·1469	·1540
12	·0888	·0946	·1005	·1066	·1128	·1193	·1259	·1327	·1396	·1468
13	·0824	·0881	·0940	·1002	·1065	·1130	·1197	·1265	·1336	·1408
14	·0769	·0826	·0885	·0947	·1010	·1076	·1143	·1213	·1284	·1357
15	·0721	·0778	·0838	·0899	·0963	·1030	·1098	·1168	·1241	·1315
16	·0679	·0736	·0796	·0858	·0923	·0989	·1059	·1130	·1203	·1278
17	·0643	·0700	·0759	·0822	·0887	·0955	·1024	·1096	·1171	·1247
18	·0610	·0667	·0727	·0790	·0855	·0924	·0994	·1067	·1142	·1219
19	·0580	·0638	·0698	·0761	·0827	·0896	·0968	·1041	·1117	·1195
20	·0554	·0612	·0672	·0736	·0802	·0872	·0944	·1018	·1095	·1175
21	·0530	·0588	·0649	·0713	·0780	·0850	·0923	·0998	·1076	·1156
22	·0509	·0566	·0627	·0692	·0760	·0830	·0904	·0980	·1059	·1140
23	·0489	·0547	·0608	·0673	·0741	·0813	·0887	·0964	·1044	·1126
24	·0471	·0529	·0590	·0656	·0725	·0797	·0872	·0950	·1030	·1113
25	·0454	·0512	·0574	·0640	·0710	·0782	·0858	·0937	·1018	·1102
26	·0439	·0497	·0559	·0626	·0696	·0769	·0846	·0925	·1007	·1092
27	·0424	·0483	·0546	·0612	·0683	·0757	·0834	·0914	·0997	·1083
28	·0411	·0470	·0533	·0600	·0671	·0746	·0824	·0905	·0988	·1074
29	·0399	·0458	·0521	·0589	·0660	·0736	·0815	·0896	·0981	·1067
30	·0387	·0447	·0510	·0578	·0651	·0726	·0806	·0888	·0973	·1061
31	·0377	·0436	·0500	·0569	·0641	·0718	·0798	·0881	·0967	·1055
32	·0367	·0426	·0490	·0560	·0633	·0710	·0791	·0875	·0961	·1050
33	·0357	·0417	·0482	·0551	·0625	·0703	·0784	·0869	·0956	·1045
34	·0348	·0408	·0473	·0543	·0618	·0696	·0778	·0863	·0951	·1041
35	·0340	·0400	·0465	·0536	·0611	·0690	·0772	·0858	·0946	·1037
36	·0332	·0392	·0458	·0529	·0604	·0864	·0767	·0853	·0942	·1033
37	·0325	·0385	·0451	·0522	·0598	·0679	·0762	·0849	·0939	·1030
38	·0318	·0378	·0445	·0516	·0593	·0674	·0758	·0845	·0935	·1027
39	·0311	·0372	·0438	·0511	·0588	·0669	·0754	·0842	·0932	·1025
40	·0305	·0366	·0433	·0505	·0583	·0665	·0750	·0839	·0930	·1023
41	·0299	·0360	·0427	·0500	·0578	·0661	·0747	·0836	·0927	·1021
42	·0293	·0354	·0422	·0495	·0574	·0657	·0743	·0833	·0925	·1019
43	·0287	·0349	·0417	·0491	·0570	·0653	·0740	·0830	·0923	·1017
44	·0282	·0344	·0412	·0487	·0566	·0650	·0738	·0828	·0921	·1015
45	·0277	·0339	·0408	·0483	·0563	·0647	·0735	·0826	·0919	·1014
46	·0272	·0335	·0404	·0479	·0559	·0644	·0733	·0824	·0917	·1013
47	·0268	·0330	·0400	·0475	·0556	·0642	·0730	·0822	·0916	·1011
48	·0263	·0326	·0396	·0472	·0553	·0639	·0728	·0820	·0915	·1010
49	·0259	·0322	·0392	·0469	·0550	·0637	·0726	·0819	·0913	·1009
50	·0255	·0318	·0389	·0465	·0548	·0634	·0725	·0817	·0912	·1009

TABLE C
CAPITAL RECOVERY FACTORS
To determine the series of "n" payments which will be yielded by a given sum invested now

Years	11%	12%	13%	14%	15%	16%	17%	18%	19%	20%
1	1·1100	1·1200	1·1300	1·1400	1·1500	1·1600	1·1700	1·1800	1·1900	1·2000
2	·5839	·5917	·5994	·6074	·6150	·6231	·6308	·6388	·6467	·6545
3	·4092	·4164	·4236	·4308	·4380	·4453	·4526	·4599	·4673	·4747
4	·3223	·3292	·3362	·3432	·3503	·3574	·3646	·3717	·3790	·3863
5	·2706	·2774	·2843	·2913	·2983	·3054	·3126	·3198	·3270	·3344
6	·2364	·2432	·2501	·2572	·2642	·2714	·2786	·2859	·2933	·3007
7	·2122	·2191	·2261	·2332	·2403	·2476	·2549	·2624	·2698	·2774
8	·1943	·2013	·2084	·2156	·2228	·2302	·2377	·2452	·2529	·2606
9	·1806	·1877	·1949	·2022	·2096	·2171	·2247	·2324	·2402	·2481
10	·1698	·1770	·1843	·1917	·1993	·2069	·2146	·2225	·2305	·2385
11	·1611	·1684	·1758	·1834	·1911	·1989	·2068	·2148	·2229	·2311
12	·1540	·1614	·1690	·1767	·1845	·1924	·2005	·2086	·2169	·2253
13	·1481	·1557	·1634	·1712	·1791	·1872	·1954	·2037	·2121	·2206
14	·1432	·1509	·1587	·1666	·1747	·1829	·1912	·1997	·2082	·2169
15	·1391	·1468	·1547	·1628	·1710	·1794	·1878	·1964	·2051	·2139
16	·1355	·1434	·1514	·1596	·1680	·1764	·1850	·1937	·2025	·2114
17	·1325	·1404	·1486	·1569	·1654	·1740	·1827	·1915	·2004	·2094
18	·1298	·1379	·1462	·1546	·1632	·1719	·1807	·1896	·1987	·2078
19	·1276	·1358	·1441	·1527	·1613	·1701	·1791	·1881	·1972	·2065
20	·1256	·1339	·1424	·1510	·1598	·1687	·1777	·1868	·1960	·2054
21	·1238	·1322	·1408	·1495	·1584	·1674	·1765	·1857	·1951	·2044
22	·1223	·1308	·1395	·1483	·1573	·1664	·1755	·1848	·1942	·2037
23	·1210	·1296	·1383	·1472	·1563	·1654	·1747	·1841	·1935	·2031
24	·1198	·1285	·1373	·1463	·1554	·1647	·1740	·1834	·1930	·2026
25	·1187	·1275	·1364	·1455	·1547	·1640	·1734	·1829	·1925	·2021
26	·1178	·1266	·1357	·1448	·1541	·1634	·1729	·1825	·1921	·2018
27	·1170	·1259	·1350	·1442	·1535	·1630	·1725	·1821	·1917	·2015
28	·1163	·1252	·1344	·1437	·1531	·1626	·1721	·1818	·1915	·2012
29	·1156	·1247	·1339	·1432	·1527	·1622	·1718	·1815	·1912	·2010
30	·1150	·1241	·1334	·1428	·1523	·1619	·1715	·1813	·1910	·2008
31	·1145	·1237	·1330	·1425	·1520	·1616	·1713	·1811	·1909	·2007
32	·1140	·1233	·1327	·1421	·1517	·1614	·1711	·1809	·1907	·2006
33	·1136	·1229	·1323	·1419	·1515	·1612	·1710	·1808	·1906	·2005
34	·1133	·1226	·1321	·1416	·1513	·1610	·1708	·1807	·1905	·2004
35	·1129	·1223	·1318	·1414	·1511	·1609	·1707	·1805	·1904	·2003
36	·1126	·1221	·1316	·1413	·1510	·1608	·1706	·1805	·1904	·2003
37	·1124	·1218	·1314	·1411	·1509	·1607	·1705	·1804	·1903	·2002
38	·1121	·1216	·1313	·1410	·1507	·1606	·1704	·1803	·1902	·2002
39	·1119	·1215	·1311	·1408	·1506	·1605	·1704	·1803	·1902	·2002
40	·1117	·1213	·1310	·1407	·1506	·1604	·1703	·1802	·1902	·2001
41	·1116	·1212	·1309	·1406	·1505	·1604	·1703	·1802	·1902	·2001
42	·1114	·1210	·1308	·1406	·1504	·1603	·1702	·1802	·1901	·2001
43	·1112	·1209	·1307	·1405	·1504	·1603	·1702	·1801	·1901	·2001
44	·1111	·1208	·1306	·1404	·1503	·1602	·1702	·1801	·1901	·2001
45	·1110	·1207	·1305	·1404	·1503	·1602	·1702	·1801	·1901	·2001
46	·1109	·1207	·1305	·1403	·1502	·1602	·1701	·1801	·1901	·2000
47	·1108	·1206	·1304	·1403	·1502	·1601	·1701	·1801	·1901	·2000
48	·1107	·1205	·1304	·1403	·1502	·1601	·1701	·1801	·1900	·2000
49	·1107	·1205	·1303	·1402	·1502	·1601	·1701	·1801	·1900	·2000
50	·1106	·1204	·1303	·1402	·1501	·1601	·1701	·1801	·1900	·2000

TABLE C
CAPITAL RECOVERY FACTORS
To determine the series of "n" payments which will be yielded by a given sum invested now

Years	21%	22%	23%	24%	25%	26%	27%	28%	29%	30%
1	1·2100	1·2200	1·2300	1·2400	1·2500	1·2600	1·2700	1·2800	1·2900	1·3000
2	·6625	·6705	·6785	·6865	·6944	·7025	·7105	·7187	·7266	·7348
3	·4822	·4897	·4972	·5047	·5123	·5199	·5275	·5352	·5429	·5507
4	·3936	·4010	·4085	·4159	·4234	·4310	·4386	·4462	·4539	·4616
5	·3417	·3492	·3567	·3642	·3719	·3795	·3872	·3949	·4027	·4106
6	·3082	·3158	·3234	·3311	·3388	·3466	·3545	·3624	·3704	·3784
7	·2851	·2928	·3006	·3084	·3163	·3243	·3324	·3405	·3486	·3569
8	·2684	·2763	·2843	·2923	·3004	·3086	·3168	·3251	·3335	·3419
9	·2561	·2641	·2723	·2805	·2888	·2971	·3056	·3140	·3226	·3312
10	·2467	·2549	·2632	·2716	·2810	·2886	·2972	·3059	·3147	·3235
11	·2394	·2478	·2563	·2648	·2735	·2822	·2910	·2999	·3087	·3177
12	·2337	·2423	·2509	·2597	·2684	·2773	·2863	·2953	·3043	·3134
13	·2292	·2379	·2467	·2556	·2646	·2736	·2826	·2918	·3010	·3102
14	·2256	·2345	·2434	·2524	·2615	·2706	·2799	·2891	·2984	·3078
15	·2228	·2317	·2408	·2499	·2591	·2684	·2777	·2871	·2965	·3060
16	·2204	·2295	·2387	·2479	·2572	·2666	·2760	·2855	·2950	·3046
17	·2185	·2277	·2370	·2464	·2558	·2652	·2747	·2843	·2939	·3035
18	·2170	·2263	·2357	·2451	·2546	·2641	·2737	·2833	·2930	·3027
19	·2158	·2252	·2346	·2441	·2537	·2633	·2729	·2826	·2923	·3021
20	·2147	·2242	·2337	·2433	·2529	·2626	·2723	·2820	·2918	·3016
21	·2139	·2234	·2330	·2426	·2523	·2620	·2718	·2816	·2914	·3012
22	·2132	·2228	·2324	·2421	·2519	·2616	·2714	·2812	·2911	·3009
23	·2127	·2223	·2320	·2417	·2615	·2613	·2711	·2810	·2908	·3007
24	·2122	·2219	·2316	·2414	·2512	·2610	·2709	·2808	·2906	·3005
25	·2118	·2215	·2313	·2411	·2510	·2608	·2707	·2806	·2905	·3004
26	·2115	·2213	·2311	·2409	·2508	·2607	·2705	·2804	·2904	·3003
27	·2112	·2210	·2309	·2407	·2506	·2605	·2704	·2804	·2903	·3002
28	·2110	·2208	·2307	·2406	·2505	·2604	·2703	·2803	·2902	·3002
29	·2108	·2207	·2306	·2405	·2504	·2603	·2703	·2802	·2902	·3002
30	·2107	·2206	·2305	·2404	·2503	·2603	·2702	·2802	·2901	·3001
31	·2106	·2205	·2304	·2403	·2503	·2602	·2702	·2801	·2901	·3001
32	·2105	·2204	·2303	·2402	·2502	·2602	·2701	·2801	·2901	·3001
33	·2104	·2203	·2303	·2402	·2502	·2601	·2701	·2801	·2901	·3001
34	·2103	·2203	·2302	·2402	·2501	·2601	·2701	·2801	·2901	·3000
35	·2103	·2202	·2302	·2401	·2501	·2601	·2701	·2801	·2900	·3000
36	·2102	·2202	·2301	·2401	·2501	·2601	·2701	·2800	·2900	·3000
37	·2102	·2201	·2301	·2401	·2501	·2601	·2700	·2800	·2900	·3000
38	·2101	·2201	·2301	·2401	·2501	·2601	·2700	·2800	·2900	·3000
39	·2101	·2201	·2301	·2400	·2501	·2600	·2700	·2800	·2900	
40	·2101	·2201	·2301	·2400	·2500	·2600	·2700	·2800		
41	·2101	·2201	·2300	·2400	·2500	·2600	·2700	·2800		
42	·2101	·2200	·2300	·2400	·2500	·2600	·2700			
43	·2101	·2200	·2300	·2400	·2500	·2600				
44	·2100	·2200	·2300	·2400	·2500					
45	·2100	·2200	·2300	·2400	·2500					
46	·2100	·2200	·2300	·2400						
47	·2100	·2200	·2300	·2400						
48	·2100	·2200	·2300							
49	·2100	·2200								
50	·2100	·2200								

TABLE C
CAPITAL RECOVERY FACTORS
To determine the series of "n" payments which will be yielded by a given sum invested now

Years	31%	32%	33%	34%	35%	36%	37%	38%	39%	40%
1	1·3100	1·3200	1·3300	1·3400	1·3500	1·3600	1·3700	1·3800	1·3900	1·4000
2	·7429	·7510	·7591	·7673	·7755	·7838	·7920	·8002	·8085	·8167
3	·5584	·5662	·5740	·5818	·5896	·5975	·6055	·6134	·6214	·6293
4	·4694	·4772	·4850	·4929	·5008	·5087	·5167	·5246	·5327	·5408
5	·4185	·4264	·4344	·4424	·4505	·4585	·4667	·4749	·4831	·4913
6	·3865	·3946	·4028	·4110	·4193	·4276	·4359	·4443	·4528	·4613
7	·3651	·3735	·3819	·3903	·3988	·4073	·4159	·4245	·4332	·4419
8	·3504	·3589	·3675	·3762	·3849	·3936	·4024	·4113	·4202	·4291
9	·3399	·3487	·3575	·3663	·3752	·3841	·3931	·4022	·4112	·4203
10	·3323	·3413	·3502	·3593	·3683	·3774	·3866	·3958	·4050	·4143
11	·3268	·3359	·3450	·3542	·3634	·3727	·3820	·3913	·4007	·4101
12	·3226	·3318	·3411	·3504	·3598	·3692	·3787	·3882	·3976	·4072
13	·3196	·3289	·3383	·3478	·3572	·3667	·3763	·3859	·3955	·4051
14	·3172	·3267	·3362	·3457	·3553	·3649	·3746	·3842	·3939	·4036
15	·3155	·3250	·3347	·3443	·3539	·3636	·3733	·3831	·3928	·4026
16	·3142	·3238	·3335	·3432	·3529	·3626	·3724	·3822	·3920	·4018
17	·3132	·3229	·3326	·3424	·3521	·3620	·3717	·3816	·3914	·4013
18	·3124	·3222	·3320	·3418	·3516	·3614	·3713	·3811	·3911	·4009
19	·3118	·3216	·3315	·3413	·3512	·3610	·3709	·3808	·3907	·4007
20	·3114	·3213	·3311	·3410	·3509	·3608	·3707	·3806	·3905	·4005
21	·3111	·3209	·3308	·3407	·3506	·3606	·3705	·3805	·3904	·4004
22	·3108	·3207	·3306	·3405	·3505	·3604	·3704	·3803	·3903	·4002
23	·3106	·3205	·3305	·3404	·3504	·3603	·3703	·3802	·3902	·4002
24	·3105	·3204	·3304	·3403	·3502	·3602	·3702	·3802	·3902	·4001
25	·3104	·3203	·3303	·3402	·3502	·3602	·3701	·3801	·3901	·4001
26	·3103	·3202	·3302	·3402	·3501	·3601	·3701	·3801	·3901	·4001
27	·3102	·3202	·3302	·3401	·3501	·3601	·3701	·3801	·3900	·4000
28	·3102	·3201	·3301	·3401	·3501	·3601	·3700	·3800	·3900	·4000
29	·3101	·3201	·3301	·3401	·3501	·3600	·3700	·3800	·3900	·4000
30	·3101	·3201	·3301	·3401	·3500	·3600	·3700	·3800	·3900	·4000
31	·3101	·3201	·3300	·3400	·3500	·3600	·3700	·3800	·3900	
32	·3101	·3200	·3300	·3400	·3500	·3600	·3700			
33	·3100	·3200	·3300	·3400	·3500	·3600				
34	·3100	·3200	·3300	·3400	·3500					
35	·3100	·3200	·3300							
36	·3100	·3200	·3300							
37	·3100									

Appendix II

Self-examination Questions

The questions which follow are closely related to the examples used in the text and should provide a useful check on understanding. In most cases, reference to the text should enable any doubts about the solution to be cleared.

1. A company has retained earnings of £5,000,000 after deducting dividends £4,900,000; tax £6,200,000; interest £9,780,000; operating costs £219,576,000; depreciation £16,666,000; and fixed asset replacement reserve £2,000,000. Calculate the cash generation.

2. What factors have stimulated the present interest in improved profitability measures?

3. Distinguish between risk, uncertainty and intangibles.

4. What is the difference between earnings and cash generation?

5. What are the requirements for (*a*) earnings, (*b*) cash generation?

6. Show in diagrammatic form the capital investment situation and give a brief explanation of it.

7. What is meant by the going-concern and the new-project evaluation?

8. Outline the main practices on the valuation of assets in company reports and accounts.

9. The following five projects are to be evaluated for relative profitability—

		A	B	C	D	E
Year 0	Capital Cost	1,000	1,000	1,000	1,000	1,000
1	Net Cash Income	500	600	1,000	—	1,000
2		500	500	—	500	500
3		500	400	—	1,000	

For each one calculate and compare—

(*a*) Comparative cost

(*b*) Pay-back

(*c*) Return on investment

i. On initial investment

ii. On average investment

(*d*) The net present value at a 10% discount rate

(*e*) The yield or internal rate of return.

10. Two projects involve the investment of £5,000. One will

return £3,000 for two years and £1,000 in the third. The second returns £10,000 in Year 3. Which is the most profitable?

11. Two projects show the following predicted results—

			PROJECT C	PROJECT D
Time 0	Net cash investment		7,580	7,580
Year 1	Cash returns	. . .	3,000	1,000
Year 2	Cash returns	. . .	2,500	1,500
Year 3	Cash returns	. . .	2,000	2,000
Year 4	Cash returns	. . .	1,500	2,500
Year 5	Cash returns	. . .	1,000	3,000
			£10,000	£10,000

Calculate the pay-back and yield of each.

12. A business man is considering buying a machine costing £1,600 which will produce a net cash flow for five years of £600 a year.

He can lease the machine for £500 a year. Is the proposition profitable and should he lease or buy?

13. The total assets of a company are as follows—

		£(000s)
Fixed assets	. .	7,400
Goodwill, etc.	. .	400
Trade investment	. .	100
Current assets	. .	6,900
		£14,800

Profits were £972,000 after adding investment income of £18,000. Current liabilities were £4,200,000 and the total equity of the ordinary shareholders is £8,200,000. The gross interest payable was £136,000; taxation took £202,000; preference share dividends were £51,000 after tax and outside shareholders took £43,000. Calculate the profitability—

(*a*) On total assets
(*b*) On total assets employed
(*c*) On assets provided by long-term funds
(*d*) On assets provided by ordinary shareholders.

14. A company invests £20,000 on which it expects to earn £6,000 per year for ten years. If it charges straight-line depreciation, what profits will it report?

15. If the project is abandoned after five years, what profits and losses will be reported if the project has no resale value at that time?

16. What would be the reported profits or losses if the equipment were sold for £2,000 at the end of five years?

17. Company A has a capitalization of £2,000,000 of which 20 per cent is raised by a debenture. Company B has the same amount of

capital but has raised £1,600,000 by debenture. What percentage borrowing does Company B have. Is it more highly geared than A? Calculate the percentage divided paid to shareholders if both debentures are entitled to 5% and profits are—

Year 1	£200,000
2	£100,000
3	£450,000

18. Outline the accounting methods of valuing stock, goodwill, fixed assets (plant, etc.).

19. What resources are omitted from a Balance Sheet?

20. What are the main limitations of published company Balance Sheets?

21. Are leased assets shown in company Balance Sheets? If not, how should they be shown? If they are shown, is the treatment satisfactory?

22. What sources of information are used in project evaluation?

23. What are the three principles of evaluation and how is each one applied?

24. Are past costs relevant to investment decisions?

25. What are the four main problems of capital budgeting?

26. What are the main categories of investment projects?

26. What are the main categories of investment projects? Which, if any, would you prefer? Are there any which you would reject altogether?

27. Define net cash investment and net cash returns.

28. A project requires fixed assets of £20,000 and stocks of £4,000. It will replace an asset which can be disposed of for £1,000. What is the net cash investment required? The sales of the product will be £40,000 per annum and there will be running costs of £30,000 per annum (including depreciation of £6,000 per annum). If tax is at the rate of 50 per cent, what will be the net cash return?

29. If the project in question 28 has a life of eight years, what rate of return does it offer? If a rate of 20 per cent is required, what is the minimum acceptable life?

30. Calculate the pay-back in the following projects and plot this on a pay-back chart.

	PROJECT A £	PROJECT B £
Time 0 Net cash investment . .	100,000	100,000
Year 1	40,000	60,000
Year 2	40,000	40,000
Year 3	40,000	25,000
Year 4	90,000	25,000
	£210,000	£150,000

31. What is the average rate of return on investment on the two projects in question 30.

32. Using the profitability index, calculate the rate of return on a project which involves an initial outlay of £4,000, followed a year later by an outlay of £6,000. There will be returns of £2,000, £6,000 and £8,000 in the three succeeding years.

33. A firm may buy a new machine for £1,000 or a secondhand one for £500. The life of the former would be five years during which time its costs will be £100 for two years, £105 for the next two years and £110 in the final year. The latter has a life of three years during which time it will cost £250 per annum to maintain. The company looks for a return of 8 per cent. Which offers the least annual cost?

34. Using the data given in question 33, what will be the decision if both the machines have a life of five years?

35. Does the going-concern method accurately measure the true yield on a company's investment? What factors give rise to the error?

36. A project requires a net cash investment of £600,000 and will return £120,000 per annum for ten years. Calculate and plot the net present value profit profile.

37. Two projects involve the investment of £800,000. One, Project X, will return a minimum of £228,000 and a maximum of £252,000 annually. The other, Project Z, will return a minimum of £332,000 and a maximum of £450,800. Project X has a life of twenty years and Project Z a life of five years. Calculate and plot the net present value cost profile.

38. An asset will cost £1,600 and it will produce returns of £600 per annum. It can be leased for £350 per annum or it can be purchased on hire purchase. In this case a deposit of one quarter of the capital must be paid. Ten per cent interest is charged on the balance which must be paid off in two years.

Is it worth while acquiring the asset and, if so, should it be bought outright, hire purchased or leased?

39. What non-financial factors affect the decision to lease or to buy on hire purchase?

40. A company can invest £12,000 in two possible ways. One way will produce £5,700 per annum for three years. The other will produce £1,953 per annum for ten years. Use whatever assumptions you may need to suggest possible lines of answer to this problem.

40. A shopkeeper is unsure which class of trade a new shop which he is building will appeal to. If he spends £50,000 he expects £21,250 per annum for three years. If he spends £65,000 he may earn £29,160 per annum over the same period. What amount would you recommend him to spend, if any?

41. Using your figures, illustrate the problems which arise and the

various approaches which may be made when a project involves capital outlays in a year after returns have already been received.

42. A company is considering the purchase of a machine for £10,000 delivered and installed. The economic life is estimated to be ten years and the cost savings which it will produce, £2,000 per annum.

The machine would replace an old one which has a physical life of twenty years.

The company borrows funds at 5 per cent and expects a return of 20 per cent before tax on its investment.

Should the company buy the proposed equipment—

(*a*) If the present equipment has no book value and no scrap value?

(*b*) If the present equipment has been depreciated at a rate of 10 per cent for four years and has a book value of £4,800 although it has no scrap value, should the company buy the new equipment?

(*c*) Suppose the present equipment's book value is £4,800 and it has a scrap value of £3,000, should it be bought?

(*d*) If the new machine will only save £1,000 a year but it will have an economic life of twenty years, should it be bought?

(*e*) Suppose the old machine has a book value of £4,800 and a scrap value of £3,000 and that the book value for tax is £3,096; the new machine will attract 20 per cent investment grant, 10 per cent initial allowance and 20 per cent annual allowance. The rate of Corporation tax is 40 per cent.

Assume that tax is payable after a delay of twelve months. Should the firm buy the new equipment?

(*f*) Supposing that the company has installed machine B, and that two years later a new machine C comes on the market which renders B obsolete so that B has no resale value. Machine C will cost £20,000 but it expected to give savings of £5,000 per annum over the cost of operating machine B. Disregard taxes. Should the firm dispose of machine A?

(*g*) Taking the Corporation tax at 40 per cent and assuming that the old machine attracted, and the new machine will attract, 20 per cent investment grant, 10 per cent initial and 20 per cent annual allowance, should machine B be replaced?

(*h*) Would your answer to question 42(*g*) be the same if the machines were sited in a Development Area and attracting investment grants of 40 per cent.

43. X Ltd. has the option of buying an office block outright for £200,000. It has an estimated economic life of sixty years. X Ltd. can also lease the same building for twenty years for an annual (end year) payment of £4,800. Either way X Ltd. is fully responsible for rates, repairs, and maintenance. If X Ltd. buys the office block, it

estimates it will be worth £120,000 in twenty years' time. The building attracts no tax allowance for ownership because it is a commercial building but the lease payments can be set off against tax. Income tax and profits tax combined equal 50 per cent. In these circumstances, assuming X Ltd. can borrow money at 8 per cent on overdraft terms for the whole period, should it lease or buy the building? Suppose there is a general inflation of 2 per cent per annum for the next twenty years—should this affect the decision? Suppose the cost of the overdraft falls to 4 per cent, will this affect the decision?

Bibliography

ALFRED, A. M. and EVANS, J. B., *Discounted Cash Flow* (London, Chapman & Hall, 1965).

ASSOCIATION OF CERTIFIED AND CORPORATE ACCOUNTANTS, *Corporation Tax* (London, 1966).

BARRISH, N., *Economic Analysis* (New York, McGraw-Hill, 1962).

BIERMAN, H. and SMIDT, S., *The Capital Budgeting Decision* (New York, Macmillan, 1960).

CASTLE, E. F. and GARBUTT, D., *Principles of Accounts* (London, U.T.P., 1962).

DEAN, J., *Capital Budgeting* (New York, Columbia University Press, 1951). *Managerial Economics* (Englewood Cliffs, N.J., Prentice-Hall, 1951).

DONALDSON, D., HUNT, P. and WILLIAMS, C. M., *Basic Business Finance* (Homewood, Illinois, R. D. Irwin Inc., 1966).

GARBUTT, D. (Ed.), *Carter's Advanced Accounts* (London, Pitman, 1962. *Profit-planning* (London, Gee & Co., 1967).

GRANT, E. L., *Principles of Engineering Economy* (New York, Ronald Press, 1964).

HUNT, P., *Financial Analysis in Capital Budgeting* (Boston, Harvard University Press, 1965).

INSTITUTE OF COST AND WORKS ACCOUNTANTS, *The Profitable Use of Capital in Industry* (London, 1965).

KINGSHOTT, L., *Investment Appraisal* (Warley, Essex, Ford Motor Co. Ltd., 1967).

MERRETT, A. J. and SYKES, A., *Capital Budgeting and Company Finance* (London, Longmans, 1966).

NATIONAL ASSOCIATION OF ACCOUNTANTS, *Return on Capital as a Guide to Managerial Decisions* (New York, 1959).

TERBORGH, G., *Dynamic Equipment Policy* (New York, McGraw-Hill, 1949).

Index